# China's Railways

# China's Railways

**Steaming into a new age**

Colin Garratt

Patrick Stephens

British Library Cataloguing in Publication Data

Garratt, Colin
    China's railways: steaming into a new age.
    1. China. Railway services
    I. Title
    385'.0951

    ISBN 0-85059-885-0

Patrick Stephens Limited is part of the
Thorsons Publishing Group, Wellingborough, Northamptonshire,
NN8 2RQ England

Printed in Great Britain by Butler and Tanner Limited, Frome, Somerset
Typeset by MJL Limited, Hitchin, Hertfordshire

10  9  8  7  6  5  4  3  2  1

# Contents

# Introduction

We dreamed of getting to China. Closed to the Western world, it was the last great enigma to anyone with an interest in railways where many ancient types of locomotive might be discovered. All kinds of rarities were to be anticipated including four-cylinder 'Mallets' barking their way through the Western Mountains and lovely 4-2-2 singles exported from Kerr Stuart's California works in Stoke-on-Trent in 1911 — surely some would still be active on a remote rural branch? There were even rumours of steam locomotives still being built and this exciting prospect served to heighten the wonder and to intensify the desire to explore this vast country. But it was all a dream, China was irretrievably closed, few nationals could leave the country and no foreign tourists were allowed in.

But then, fortunately, came changes in China's attitude to the rest of the world. The 'opening up' pioneered by Chinese leader Deng Xiaoping in many forms enabled this last great treasure house of steam traction to be investigated and the first groups of foreigners interested in railways were able to penetrate the country. Initially they were coerced into seeing the attainments of the revolution: hospitals, kindergartens and schools — even, on at least one occasion, a peoples' laundry — but some glimpses of the railway were afforded and by 1980 reports of steamlined Manchurian 'Pacifics' and Edwardian-built Dubs 'Moguls' filtered into the Western railway press, along with a plethora of traditional American traction spiced with latter-day Russian practice. 'Behind the Bamboo Curtain' a whole new railway system opened up: a system rich in history, vast in geographical distribution, and dynamic in its importance to the country it served, for it was soon revealed that China's railways were the heartbeat of the economy. Furthermore, the railway revolution was far from complete, with many lines still being constructed. China was, perhaps, the last true 'railway based economy' on earth.

Prior to my first visit in 1983 I expected to experience feelings of wonder for the railway, but reserve about the people. China was a truly 'foreign' nation: unlike many other countries I have visited the British had exerted little influence on its development, either economically or historically. It was an alien culture. Having worked extensively in India, with all its British connections, I expected to feel uncharacteristic isolation and remove amid a people strange in appearance and at such variance culturally. How wrong I was to be. Within hours of arriving in Beijing I became aware of the beauty of the Chinese people, a beauty both of disposition and appearance. For here in this teeming land, with one quarter of the human race within its borders — over a billion people — I found cleanliness, orderliness, discipline and elegance.

On that first trip I headed eastwards from the capital city, Beijing, through Manchuria to discover a railway system whose strength and virility matched those of Britain at the height of the railway age. Every small station had its goods sheds and sidings intact, pick-up freights vied with heavy long distance freight hauls bearing every conceivable commodity and all fitted in between a fine variety of fast and semi-fast passenger services. But, to cap it all, as if that were not exciting enough, the greater majority of trains were worked by steam.

Upon reaching Shenyang we were met by a representative of the China International Travel Service (CITS). The journey to our hotel was several miles and whilst driving through the bleak streets dusted lightly with snow, we passed only one other car along with the odd lorry, a few light trucks and the occasional jeep. Traffic was almost non-existent. I was already sensing a tranquillity in Chinese society which came as a total contrast to the cut and thrust tumble so familiar in the Western democracies.

Perhaps the spirit of the China we found then is best summed up by an incident in the steel capital Anshan, when, having booked into our hotel and left several thousand pounds worth of photographic equipment littered around the bedroom floor, we found that there was no key to the room. Requesting one from reception brought the reply that they had no key and neither was one necessary — our equipment would be safe! Of course, it was, and that simple event sums up everything that every Western visitor admires in China. Whatever the traumas and tragedies incurred during Mao's communist revolution of 1949, his vision has clearly built a society of remarkable unity with each individual working for the state, which, in turn, has fed, housed, clothed, and hospitalized a burgeoning population.

Today, news of reform dances across the pages of the Chinese press. Now the happiness of the people is the major goal: a happiness to be achieved through economic and material prosperity. Experiments with stock exchanges, money markets, free marketing and house buying have begun and foreign investors are encouraged. All this, combined with freer speech and a freer press, is unleashing powerful new forces, not all of which are necessarily directed to the common good. It is becoming increasingly evident that Western techniques can't be divorced from a free-wheeling competitive environment. Unfettered transition from socialism to capitalism is one thing, but the market socialism that China is aiming for — a fanciful half-way house in which market and planned private and public properties peacefully co-exist — presents a formidable challenge.

The opening up to the West has inevitably led to a noisier and brasher culture. Every visitor I have ever taken to China with the groups that I lead through the Occidor travel company has expressed fear for the traditional beauty and naïvety of these great people. Personal gain is becoming ever more evident, manifested most obviously in the money touts who stalk the streets of Beijing and other major centres.

Sadly, China now talks of road development, showing that she is capable of importing even the most pernicious of Western diseases. Into a country devoid of motorways, family motor cars and indeed with few juggernaut lorries, comes talk of major trunk road building, perhaps the first sign of a shift away from a traditional railway economy. How a nation blessed with a population of over one billion could turn, even in part, to a road-based economy is bewildering, but if unfettered commercial interests are allowed to operate in China the prospects are depressing. Western influences may well ensure that this does come about. If it does, inevitably, a bottomless pit of wealth will have to be rifled to develop a transport system which, from the outset, is unviable.

But all of this, if it ever happens, is a long way away. China remains, for the present, *the* country of railways and a country of charm, dignity and great beauty. As the clouds of change gather on every horizon though, I can't help but contrast developments — for better or worse — with my impressions on that first winter visit back in 1983. The country's leaders inch their way towards economic liberalization and as they do so the country responds ever more dynamically. Almost everywhere one can see that China, as a nation, is now developing the unstoppable motion and activity more frequently associated with a powerhouse of the Western economies such as New York.

In this brief introduction to a great nation, its people and its railways I invite you to come with us to an astonishing land. China, however, will remain an enigma, even to those of us who have visited many times. Leaving the plane, one steps into a land so immense and so different from Western cultures that any form of understanding seems impossible to grasp. China stands at a historical crossroads of epic proportions and is today more fascinating than ever. Its railway system presents a staggering spectacle and an astonishing picture that sometimes mirrors changes in the nation itself. Let me introduce you then to the railways of China.

Colin Garratt
Newton Harcourt
Leicestershire
June 1988

# Chapter 1

# China - a welcome

Each year I take at least one group of visitors to see China and her railways. The overall journey time from England in Swissair luxury is nineteen hours and this time can seem like a holiday within itself as our travellers get away from the busy demands of everyday life. There is time to think, not least about the wonders which await us. Our departure from London Heathrow is at 8.30 a.m. and we arrive in Beijing at 11.15 a.m. the following day — China being seven hours ahead of GMT.

From the minute we step down from the plane China presents two challenges: firstly to gain a perspective on so vibrant a nation, and, secondly, how to respond to the pace of life in this remarkable country. Work and time are of paramount importance and in so burgeoning a land every minute seems to count. Proof of this comes immediately after our arrival, for having passed through customs, we meet our local and national guides who are waiting with a minibus to take us to the Ming tombs and onwards to the Great Wall, *before* going to our hotel in Beijing! Any thoughts of a lost night's sleep evaporate, as the fascinations of such a dramatically different culture assert themselves.

Threading through the suburbs of Beijing the modernity of China impresses many members of the party. Wherever one looks there seems to be new construction and there is little evidence of the ornate Chinese architecture that one expects to see. The bicycle is omni-present, millions of them, and at some of the traffic lights it is a case of bicycle jams rather than traffic jams in the Western sense, kindling memories of the days when the bicycle was pre-eminent in Britain as the logical adjunct of public transport. But we are bound for the Western hills, where at the head of a remote valley most of the Ming dynasty emperors lie buried.

Approaching this vast valley in all its remoteness evokes a tremendous sense of history. It is easy to imagine the long colourful processions of the imperial entourage years ago, trekking its way from Peking. We approach the tombs through the valley of the animals, a valley lined

*The dream of visiting China finally becomes a reality.*

with huge marble creatures on each side of the road, until they give way to warlike warriors, all there to guard the emperors' eternal sleep. Our visit is necessarily short but the various buildings through which we enter the tombs provide an incomparable insight into the beauty of classic Chinese architecture: its form, its colour and significance.

The Great Wall is the big attraction though and it is less than an hour's drive from the Ming tombs. To stand on the Great Wall of China — one of the seven wonders of the world — is for many in the group, almost as important as seeing the railway. Building began in the fifth century BC and by 221 BC various sections of the wall were joined to span some 2,000 miles (3,200 km), embracing valleys, deserts and mountain ranges alike, some of the most inhospitable terrain on earth being encompassed. Later fortified under the Ming dynasty, the wall became sufficiently wide for six horsemen to ride abreast. China's wall is the only one of man's creations which can be seen clearly from the moon and the building of the wall tells a lot of the indomitable spirit of the Chinese.

We reach the wall at Badaling, the most frequented spot for tourists from the capital city, but it is not difficult to appreciate the wildness. Walking along the parapet, which sometimes cants at a 45° angle, for half a mile or so, enables one to lose the crowds and to view the wall curving over the mountains for a vast distance ahead in varying states of decay. The wall's purpose was to protect the middle kingdom from invaders from the north and west.

Flushed with excitement, the group reassembles for tea before boarding our minibus for the forty-mile journey back to Beijing. Already the sun has disappeared, but the veiled lighting of the hill country keeps our sense of wonder at fever pitch. It is dark by the time we reach Beijing and now our local guide informs us that the hotel is on the opposite side of the city, a drive of some thirty miles! We enter endless miles of wide and busy thoroughfares: early evening activity in Beijing is intense and yet the city still exudes an overall sense of calm. Is it the stabilizing weight of China's timeless history?

Our hotel, far from being an ornamental edifice located in a flower garden — as our group might have believed before their arrival that morning — is a multi-storey block of concrete, built within the last three months as part of China's avid attempt to cater for the vast tourist influx that it hopes to encourage.

*After nineteen hours travelling the 'Occidor' group arrives in Beijing for the railway adventure of a lifetime.*

*The exhilaration of walking on China's Great Wall can be sensed in this scene half a mile to the east of Badaling.*

We have now travelled almost non-stop since leaving Heathrow 28 hours previously, but this is China: 'dinner in fifteen minutes' our local guide announces to the group assembled in the lobby. And he means it, for the restaurant will be closed within the hour. Fortunately our cases have arrived intact from the airport and a hurried wash and change finds the group seated round the huge circular table on which ten dishes of hors d'oeuvres are placed. Not a knife and fork in sight; neither is anyone likely to ask for them, for no matter how great a fan of Sheffield one might be, eating with chop-sticks is a delightful and extremely relaxing experience and part of coming to grips with the country. It is not an experience easily mastered but it is one which, as the tour progresses, will become a source of increasing delight. Though modern, the hotel incorporates elements of traditional China in its decor, while the sales counters are full of such delights as jade carvings, hand-coloured prints in scroll form, jewellery, fans, silk ware and rugs and carpets of exquisite quality. In culinary matters bottles of exotic fruits vie with packets of tea, arrays of boiled sweets and huge bottles of Ginseng.

Most members of the group convene in the little bar before going to bed. It is hard to believe that we are really in China, but the adventure is yet to begin. Our national guide comes to announce breakfast tomorrow morning at 7.30 and departure from the lobby at 8.30. Our destination? Tian An Men Square and the Forbidden City in the heart of Beijing.

Tian An Men Square occupies almost a hundred acres. Its name comes from the gate and tower on the north side which gives entry to the Forbidden City, the seat of China's Imperial Emperors over many long centuries. It was from the North Gate that Chairman Mao proclaimed the founding of the People's Republic of China in 1949 and when he died over a million people gathered in the square to pay homage. This gate, with its great artistic and historical importance is the national emblem of China today and a magnificent portrait of Mao gazes from the ramparts across the square. Despite the recent moves towards liberalization, Mao remains a guiding force in the country's destiny. Possibly the most memorable aspect of Tian An Men Square in fact is his mausoleum, a vast imposing building in which the embalmed body of a man who could perhaps be described as *the greatest* political leader of the 20th century lies for all to see, draped with the red flag of the communist party of China and preserved in a crystal coffin.

Bounding the square is the Great Hall of the People and the museums of 'the revolution' and of Chinese history. In the centre of the square stand monuments to the heroes of the revolution — and us, taking it all in. Tian An Men Square is a breathtakingly beautiful and inspiring place to visit and more than anywhere else seems to represent the heart of China.

All too soon we walk on through The Gate of Heavenly Peace and into the Forbidden City itself, the buildings of which date back to the beginning of the Ming dynasty. It was within this walled site that emperors ruled in grand seclusion, surrounded by their priests, ministers, concubines and eunuchs. Twenty-four emperors of the last imperial dynasties, the Ming and Qing, lived and held their courts within the Forbidden City. They controlled China with absolute rule for almost five centuries until the last dynasty fell in 1911. The half-mile walk from the North to the South Gate, through this, China's greatest architectural treasure, is a paradise for photographers. There is a sense of

*Tian An Men Square in the heart of Beijing. Notice Chairman Mao's portrait above the entrance to the Forbidden City. Either side of the portrait are the words 'Long live the People's Republic of China'.*

**Above** *Crowds wait patiently in Tian An Men Square to visit Mao's mausoleum.*

**Right** *The heroes of the Revolution depicted in granite as part of the monument to the heroes of the people in Tian An Men Square.*

**Above** *A scene from within the Forbidden City looking towards the North Gate.*

**Right** *Handle designs from one of the Forbidden City's huge bronze cauldrons.*

*Few foreign visitors fail to be captivated by the physical beauty of the Chinese. Even Europeans, attractive in their own society, often look ungainly and awkward amongst the Chinese.*

harmony between the buildings and their surroundings, a harmony too in the buildings themselves, a harmony all-pervading. In addition to the palaces and pavilions, many works of art are displayed in the different museums. The Forbidden City's grandeur impresses itself upon Chinese and foreign visitors alike and it is, perhaps, at this point, amid the breathtaking surroundings, that the beauty of the Chinese people themselves impresses itself on the group for the first time. Most are simply dressed and lead relatively frugal lives, but they exude an inner tranquillity and an outward physical beauty which becomes increasingly apparent the longer one stays in China.

Lunch now in one of the city's celebrated dumpling restaurants, before continuing to another of the city's jewels, The Temple of Heaven. Each year the emperor would visit this temple to spend the night fasting and praying in the Hall of Prayer for Good Harvest. He would also take upon himself the sins of his people and would prostrate himself as a sacrifice to his father for the redemption of mankind. His entourage would leave the Forbidden City and throughout the route every gate and window which overlooked his passage would be closed. No foreigners could watch the procession and so sacred was the occasion that trains were forced to a standstill for many hours to prevent a disturbance to the ceremony. The approach is down a tree-lined avenue at the end of which the temple, its deep blue tiles glinting in the sun-

*This scene from Beijing's Free Market indicates that despite the tremendous influx of tourists, the Chinese still remain fascinated by foreign visitors.*

light, rises up in all its majestic splendour.

Once again it is a photographer's feast, but my favourite vantage point is from the top of an adjacent hill, which, though difficult to climb, provides a superb vantage point overlooking the temple in the foreground and set against a vast modern backdrop of Beijing. It is said that this hill is formed of earth dug from Mao's underground shelter in the event of a nuclear attack. Each year, we make it a custom to meet on this hilltop for a final photographic celebration of this most sacred shrine.

Already it is past 3 o'clock and time forbids an opportunity to see the Summer Palace with its beautiful lake and gardens, so reminiscent of the China of story books. It was to this palace that the emperors would go to seek relief from the high humidity of summer.

Having gained a hint of China's history and having at least partially acclimatized, thoughts inevitably turn to the railway for we are after all, first and foremost, railway people. But our guides want to show us one of Beijing's free markets, in which private enterprise now flourishes. Afterwards, they add, we will go to Beijing railway station. It seems a reasonable compromise and soon we are lost amid the fascinating displays of a vast fruit and vegetable market, with every conceivable type of product for sale. Vendors compete avidly in setting out their stalls in the most attractive manner and the basic prin-

*Beijing's main railway station reveals the importance of China's railways and reflects the monumental treatment given to great stations throughout the world in the 19th century.*

ciple seems to be, that he who can shout loudest does the most business. This aspect of China's free market economy surprises many members of the group, who are unable to equate such colourful entrepreneurial spirit with their expectations of a country which remains essentially communist. But economic reforms have resulted in many such areas of the economy being, in effect, controlled by free enterprise and these markets now play a supplementary role to the state-run sectors. Our Chinese guides admit that they have greatly eased the production and distribution of many commodities.

Beijing railway station is one of the city's ten major buildings. It is of traditional architectural style, with symmetrical clock towers forming the centre piece and outer wings topped with tall glazed turrets. The station forecourt is a swarming mass of humanity, whilst the waiting halls and concourse are literally overflowing. Traffic has increased dramatically and passenger volume is some 250 per cent greater than it was in the early 1960s. Imposing as the station is — for entering it is not unlike the feeling one gains upon entering a large international airport — it still cannot meet the massive demands of a rapidly expanding China. Now, a new railway station is under construction at Fengtai in south-west Beijing near the vast marshalling yards, which act as a mighty clearing house for freight converging on Beijing bound for all parts of the provinces and the country. Although a largely diesel operated activity we make a note to visit Fengtai, where a 34-track humping yard serves five different main lines.

One hour spent on Beijing station is living proof of China's complete dependence on railways and it is wonderful to watch all the traditional activities associated with the departure of long distance trains. Heavy expresses loaded to twenty coaches — often with two huge diesel locomotives at their head — arrive and depart on phenomenally long

*China on the move. Travellers in the teeming waiting halls at Beijing Station.*

*The girl attendant waits to welcome passengers aboard coach No 20, on a Beijing — Zhikuai — Wuchang express.*

journeys and such is the intensity of activities that our guide proudly announces that one train arrives or departs every eight minutes through 24 hours a day, seven days a week. Unfortunately though, little steam is to be seen anywhere in Beijing.

Our appetites whetted by the sheer intensity of rail operations in China, we return to our hotel, safe in the knowledge that the next morning we are to begin our journey from Beijing north eastwards into Manchuria, one of China's most industrialized regions and the finest area of steam traction operation on earth. As one of our group so aptly says upon arrival at the hotel, 'If we were to go home now our tour would have been worth it, and we haven't seen any steam trains yet!'

# Chapter 2

# 11,000 steam locomotives at work

China was not full of the exotic rareties that we had dreamed of. In fact she has very few locomotives more than fifty years old and of the estimated total of some 11,000 active examples, around 90 per cent can be accounted for by six basic types. Considering the density of railway operations in China, only Russia has approached such a remarkable degree of standardization. Railways came to China relatively late and many important lines were built during the 20th century. Particularly extensive building has been undertaken since the founding of the People's Republic in 1949 and this has been based on standard types.

If such standardization makes the prospective visitor to China wary he need have no fear. For the full-blooded action is in the very finest of railway traditions and although many of the most exciting lines see only three different types or even less, the embellishments which the Chinese apply to their locomotives make every passing train a delightfully different experience. Polished boiler bands, stars and large colourful rectangular plates above the buffer beams — along with a wide variety of painting styles — make for a visual and photographic feast.

The principal freight types to be found on active duties are the 'QJ' Class 'Advance Forward' 2-10-2 of which some 4,500 are known to be in service; the smaller 'JS' Class 'Construction' 2-8-2 with upwards of 1,750 in service; the older 'JF' Class 'Liberation' 2-8-2 with some 1,500 at work and the 'SY' Class 'Aiming High' 2-8-2 industrial, also with 1,500 or so in service. Passenger locomotives are comprised of two basic types: the 'SL6' 'Pacific' 4-6-2 and the more recent 'RM' 'Pacific' which, between them, account for another thousand locomotives, thus bringing the total of the six main classes to approximately 9,250.

China's locomotives bear evidence of a tremendous American influence, both structurally and in terms of appearance. Much of this influence was derived secondhand through Japan, the United States having equipped that country's railroads early in the 20th century. Japanese occupation of the vast industrialized region of Manchuria in the 1930s saw the influence passed directly to China, when locomotives were built for China in both Japan and in Chinese works as well. Following the founding of the People's Republic and subsequent technical liaison with Russia up until the late 1950s, early '60s, Russian practice made its mark on China's locomotives. These influences however tend to be somewhat secondary, or cosmetic, for the underlying American strain predominates, as indeed it has in Russia itself as a result of extensive American exports to that country during the earlier phases of railway development.

The most dramatic evolution of American and Russian practice occurs with the 'QJs'. The numbers built suggest standardization along Russian lines although the 'QJs' total pales somewhat when compared with the USSR's 'E' Class 0-10-0 of which over 10,000 examples were built. The 'QJ' is China's principal freight locomotive, one engine being capable of lifting trains of up to 3,000 tons over easily graded routes, whilst hauls of 3,000 tons and more with two 'QJs' are common on lines with steeper gradients. First introduced in 1957, the 'QJs' were derived from the Soviet Railways' 'LV' Class 2-10-2, themselves derived from an American design, and they were built with Soviet technical aid. The 'QJ' design includes such Russian attributes as external main steam pipes from the dome to superheater as well as a Worthington-type feed water heater and a Delta trailing truck.

The 'QJs' have been built in six different works in China, but since the mid '60s production has been concentrated at Datong. The type has a cylinder diameter no less than 25.6 in (64 cm) with a 31.5 in (79 cm) stroke; driving wheel diameter is 4 ft 11 in (147 cm) and tractive effort is 63,340 lb. The 'QJs' have a grate area of 70 sq ft (6.5 sq m) and are mechanically stoked since no fireman could physically keep up when the locomotives are working under heavy steam. However, in practice, hand firing is not infrequent since the crews can earn a fuel-saving bonus. With three men on the engine the fireman and assistant driver take turns in hand firing, augmenting their efforts with limited use of the stoker at periods of maximum exertion. Some 'QJs' have twelve-wheeled tenders, with a coal carrying capacity of 21½ tons.

By far the most numerous steam design left on earth today, the 'QJs' are absolutely superb to see in action. In many ways they may be thought of as a rather large British Railways '9F' Class 2-10-0 yet they are infinitely more exciting, more powerful and get their heavy freight trains on the move with a stately momentum never experienced in the smaller Class '9F'. By comparison with American tradition however, the QJs' power output is modest, their tractive effort being equivalent to a typical American freight hauler of the 1930s!

The 'QJ' has been built over a period of more than thirty years and with few significant changes to the basic design. This in itself is remarkable, but consider the extensive double heading which occurs, and one is reminded of a similar policy adopted by Britain's Midland Railway over many years on its Nottinghamshire to London coal trains. Whatever deficiencies may exist in the practice of double heading and in using such an old design, the Chinese say that standardization of

*A lively scene on the coaling roads at Changchun Depot with a 'JF' Class 2-8-2 on the left and 'QJ' Class 2-10-2 on the right.*

parts and familiarity with the machinery throughout the country is a huge plus economically — as it must have been on the Midland Railway. Rather than go to the considerable expense and complexity of producing new or heavily modified designs, China stayed with the 'QJ', resisting any temptation to diversify. Particularly in a centralized economy, such a policy has doubtless reaped many rewards.

The 'QJ's smaller sisters are the standard 'JS' Class 'Mikado' locomotives. Although considerably smaller, their overall appearance is similar and from a distance it is sometimes difficult to differentiate between the two. The 'JS' Class engines perfectly illustrate the 'hybrid' development of Chinese locomotive design, in that their frames and cylinders are virtually identical to the earlier 'JF' Class which was built by the

American Locomotive Company (Alco) for the South Manchurian Railway during World War 1. The 'Mikado' received popular acceptance in America before the First World War and it is fascinating to note that the Chinese are still producing 'JS' Class engines descended directly from everyday American practice of three quarters of a century ago. The 'JS' boiler, however, represents a switch from American to Russian practice and in common with the 'QJ' this vital part of a steam locomotive has an external main steam pipe and Worthington-type feed water heater. The skyline casing of the boiler thus renders the 'JS' similar to its larger relation. The addition of windshields similar to those sported by the 'QJs' is another departure from American practice.

Evolution has rendered the proportions of the 'JS' relatively modest and the type is found today on tripping, shunting and branch line work, or acting as pilots to 'QJs' over short steeply graded sections. Another interesting analogy with British practice, and a contrast to that given above in the context of the 'QJs', is that the tractive effort of 49,000 lb offered by the 'JS' locomotives is considerably above that of the Class '9F' 2-10-0, Britain's heaviest mineral hauler!

The 'JS' Class 2-8-2s make for an extremely handsome 'Mikado' when seen with their Russian style boiler mountings, smoke deflectors and multitude of embellishments, but the reality of their origin was demonstrated very dramatically upon seeing one in industrial service, shorn of all adornments; it was purely and simply a typical American 'Mikado'.

These sentiments bring us to the 'JF' itself, a classic in locomotive evolution. Following its 1918 introduction from Alco, the type was built in prolific numbers with detail alterations during the Japanese occupation of the 1930s. Building was undertaken in Japan by such makers as Kawasaki, KSK, Hitachi and Nippon, whilst in China the type was produced by the South Manchurian Railway works in Dalian and Qingdao. Building continued from Japan well after the liberation, presumably in the form of war reparations.

With well over 2,000 of the type in existence they were a natural for adoption by the Chinese as a national class and building continued until 1957 when, following detail modifications the final form of the 'JF' provided the blueprint for the Class 'JS', the first of which appeared from Dalian that year. Though powerful and highly capable engines, the 'JFs' are also now relegated to secondary work, primarily shunting, but they are to be found in many parts of the Chinese railway system. Unlike the newer 'JS' Class, they are seldom found in line service, although evidence of their prowess can be glimpsed when they are seen engaged in heavy shunting movements in some of the bigger yards. Here one engine will move several thousand tons and their deep throaty exhaust beats literally shake the ground. Though blessed with relatively few decorative trims, some are maintained in resplendent condition. They are extremely handsome and well proportioned locomotives. In top condition, with that delightful aura of vintage, they are particularly pleasing to the eye. Equally, when seen grubby and run down, as many are today, their classic lineage shines through undiminished. They give the appearance of weary workhorses from a bygone age eking out their final days, complete with wheezing steam leaks and banging motion.

Watching 'JFs' at work, one is reminded of the heyday of American railroads, for these 'light Mikes', as the Americans called such engines, were to be found in vast numbers in many American states.

*This 'JS' Class 2-8-2 shorn of its skyline casting, smoke deflectors and front-plate reveals its pure American ancestry.*

*'JF' Class 'Mikado' No 2422 has been the shed pilot at Changchun for some years. Notice that she has an improvised coal bunker instead of the normal tender to facilitate movements within the restricted confines of the depot yard.*

They were fine haulers for heavy slogging loads over medium rail while versions with bigger driving wheels worked faster freights, for the 'Mikado' is not just a 'Consolidation' (2-8-0) with a trailer truck, but rather a distinct development aimed at improved riding and tracking qualities and unrestricted furnace proportions. This latter is achieved because the extra pair of wheels allows a deeper fire box and a longer boiler tube length.

Another world classic is, of course, the 'Pacific', the 4-6-2 wheel arrangement so often favoured by crack express locomotives. China has two splendid examples left in regular service: the 'SL6' Class of 1933 and the later, more modern, 'RM' Class introduced in 1957. The 'Pacific' was pioneered in America during the early years of the century as a fusion between the 4-6-0 and the 'Atlantic' 4-4-2. It found favour in many parts of the world and in innumerable designs, many of them highly flamboyant, and almost invariably representing the ultimate in express passenger traction. Apart from China, only India and areas of French Indo-China retain the last examples of this classic type.

The 'SL6s' were introduced for the Manchurian National Railway in 1933 and later appeared on the South Manchurian Railway too. They were built both in Japan and China with production continuing after the communist revolution until some 500 examples were in traffic.

The 'SL6' experienced a similar metamorphosis to that which

**Right** *A 'QJ' Class 2-10-2 backs up to the water column at Harbin shed on a misty winter's morning in a temperature of minus 30° centigrade.*

**Below** *The handsome form of 'SL6' Class 'Pacific' No 627 enlivens the Ash Disposal Pits at Harbin shed. It is summer 1986 and she has worked in from Jilin on the last regular steam-hauled passenger turn in the Harbin area.*

produced the 'JF' Class, in that the 'RM' 'Pacific' introduced from Sifang in 1957 used the same frame and cylinders but a Russian design of boiler. This boiler is almost certainly identical to that on the 'JS' 'Mikado'. Building of 'RMs' continued until 1961 and the type became a standard long distance express passenger locomotive in many parts of China. Dieselization of a number of areas has ousted them from the top duties, not least because the phenomenally long distance passenger trains of more recent years have rendered them too weak for such roles. Nevertheless they are still found, particularly throughout Manchuria, on a wide range of secondary and cross-country passenger services.

Both classes are superb engines to behold and with a driving wheel diameter of 5 ft 9 in (1.75 m) they are sufficiently racy looking to represent their lineage admirably. At the same time the multitude of adornments and embellishments produces a tremendous variety of different guises.

There is one other 'Pacific' which occasionally sees main line service. The 'SL7' Class streamliner was originally introduced for working the air-conditioned Asia high-speed express between Dalian and Shenyang, or Mukden as it was then known. This luxury train achieved worldwide publicity and was fully in keeping with the streamlined era of the 1930s; it was the epitome of luxury rail travel and the engine's design was similar to the New York Central's 'K5' 'Pacifics' on the famous Mercury express. This magnificent engine is one of the few streamlined

*A contrasting scene in warm autumn sunlight depicting three 'QJs' under the sand hoppers situated alongside the ash disposal pits at Harbin Locomotive Shed.*

*The yard of Harbin Tram Shed, during its final days of operation.*

'Pacifics' to survive in running order; she has a driving wheel diameter of 6 ft 6¾ in (2 m) and is a reminder of a flamboyant epoch in the evolution of the steam locomotive which captured the imaginations of people worldwide. Seeing an 'SL7' in action, one is reminded of the way in which thousands of people were drawn to the tracksides to see such technological wonders in those halcyon pre-television years. It is not surprising that today's diesel-hauled services between Dalian and Shenyang are both slower and less comfortable.

So ends our review of China's five principal main line designs. Many fascinating non-standard types survived in traffic until recent years, in many cases until the late '70s, the most obvious example being the Soviet Railways 'FD' Class 2-10-2s introduced in 1931. Some 1,250 of these were transferred to China under the Sino-Soviet technical Co-operation pact and were re-gauged from Russia's 5 ft to the Chinese standard (4 ft 8½ in). A few still survive in areas south of the Yangtse whilst derelict examples are to be found in various parts of the system — some relegated to stationary boiler duties. Quite a number of interesting main line classes were pensioned off to industrial service during the '60s and '70s, but as we shall see later the introduction of the standard industrial design, the 'SY' Class, has all but ousted these.

Perhaps the best centre for appreciating the diversity of China's locomotive heritage is Shenyang, where the main depot at Su ja Tun

*Action on the ash disposal pits at Harbin Depot with a 'JS' Class 2-8-2 left and 'QJ' Class 2-10-2 right.*

has an allocation of over 100 locomotives and examples of 'QJ', 'JS', 'JF' and both designs of 'Pacific' can all be seen. In addition and adjacent to Su ja Tun, is the nucleus of China's first railway museum, which at present consists of a long line of some twenty locomotives in varying states of decay. The collection includes a Russian 'FD' and a 'JF2', one of 27 magnificent three-cylinder 2-8-2s complete with Gresley-conjugated valve gear which were delivered by Alco to the South Manchurian Railway in 1924. Railway visitors from Japan and the West have obviously helped to persuade the Chinese that it is worth taking some care of their railway history. The authorities at this budding National Railway Museum show great keenness in exhibiting and restoring the locomotives and there seems little doubt that, in the foreseeable future, the Shenyang collection will turn into a superbly constituted museum.

For the present, developments at the museum pale to insignificance when compared with the activities at the neighbouring Su ja Tun shed, where the intensity of the coaling, watering, fire-raking and sanding operations remain in the finest of steam railway traditions.

# Chapter 3

# On the great steam main lines

The stopping train from Yingkou to Changchun draws into Shenyang station and the members of our group take their seats in the soft class. It is September 1986 and we are bound for Changchun. Our train leaves on time at 12 o'clock precisely and within minutes we have passed several 'JFs' engaged in heavy shunting, whilst on a 'QJ' held in the yard with a southbound freight we see a fireman vigorously polishing the works plate and boiler bands, recalling the traditional pride of footplate crews the world over. Threading through the industrial suburbs complete with belching chimneys, I am reminded of my travels through industrial Britain during the 1950s.

Eventually we head out onto the double track main line and our 'DFH 3' diesel works the sixteen-coach train up to a customary cruising speed of 50 mph (80.5 kph). Suddenly there is an explosion of sound and a 'QJ' flashes past the window with a long southbound freight, the closing speed of the two trains being at least 100 mph (161 kph). Minutes later, another southbound train, this one behind two 'QJs', brings the excitement of the group to fever pitch; we really are back in the age of steam! In between passing freights the landscape unfolding beyond our windows is there to be enjoyed. It is densely farmed, almost every piece of usable land being given over to agriculture. There is sadly little evidence of birds or any other kind of wildlife.

Within the hour our group is called to the dining car, where, for 10 yuan — a little over £2 — a multitude of steaming hot dishes are set before us. One always looks forward to meals when travelling by rail in China, because the food is appetizing, freshly cooked and piping hot. On this occasion, our medium-priced repast consists of dishes of celery and pork, prawns in tomato sauce, battered meat balls, battered pork served with a huge bowl of rice and followed by egg soup, and all enhanced with a very palatable local beer. But lunch is no break from the pleasure of the railway operation. At a wayside station we pass a 'QJ' shunting wagonloads of agricultural produce often brought directly to the railhead by horse-drawn cart.

Returning to our seats from the dining car our flasks are filled with boiling water by the attendant for after dinner tea or coffee. These hot water flasks are one of the many delights of rail travel in China. Coal-fired boilers are located throughout the train to provide water for tea, often drunk continuously throughout the long journeys. The early autumn sun, shining from a clear blue sky, has begun to dip slightly by the time we reach Kai-yuan at 14.30, uncharacteristically 35 minutes late! Rail travel in China is not fast, even the better expresses average little more than 50 mph (80.5 kph), but more often they are punctual to the second and this was one of the few occasions I have ever known a train in China to be late. As the train runs late into the station a cry goes up 'JF6', which brings the entire group to the windows and straining to see one of the last examples of this superb, but now elusive, 'Mikado' locomotive ending its days on shunting duties. Two more of the type are seen derelict in the shed yard.

Continuing northwards the sunlight becomes ever more golden, the afternoon ever more sleepy. Some members are following maps of the journey, but most keep an ever-watchful eye on the line, never tiring of the succession of southbound freights which, chime whistles screaming, roar past in such an alarming way. Our next main stop is Changtu where an immaculate 'JF', No 2411, is on yard shunt. She brings whistles and gasps of appreciation from all members of the party, as she stands with gleaming brass boiler bands and freshly painted box-pok driving wheels enjoying a brief siesta between bouts of shunting. She is one of a batch built in China during the 1950s and thus actually far newer than her design and lineage suggest.

Further north still, we pass a stream of colourful flowers planted in straight lines by the track sides. Large sections of China's main lines are so bedecked and they add a vibrant band of colour in an otherwise relatively colourless landscape. Then we catch sight of a 'Pacific'. Fortuitously we are at a point where the up and down lines diverge to cross a river over separate open top bridges and approaching on the southbound line comes an 'RM' at speed, at the head of a fourteen-coach passenger train. With grey smoke swirling from its chimney and with large driving wheels spinning gloriously she is every bit the

*Admission ticket to China's first railway museum in Shenyang.*

沈 阳 铁 路 蒸 汽 机 车 陈 列 馆

参　观　券

沈 阳　铁 路
蒸汽机车陈列馆

每券一人　　　开馆时间　10.00～15.00

thoroughbred personified, magnificently displaying the full dignity of the 'Pacific'.

Soon we are running into Siping, one of the larger towns on our route and the half way point for Shenyang and Changchun locomotives. It is here that the 'QJs' operating the long distance freights change over. The Shenyang engines give way to those that work in from Changchun and in the huge sheds intense servicing operations are carried out under a permanent mushroom of dark smoke. Siping provides some thrills too, for no sooner have we drawn to a halt than a 'QJ' arrives from the north with a passenger train. These engines are not commonly seen in passenger service, the 'Pacifics' being the preferred motive power, the 'QJ' being a rough locomotive to ride at speed. The 'QJ' draws to a halt as a southbound freight races through the station at speed. With whistles blaring on both locomotives to add to the noise, the roar of the wagons in the confined space is deafening as the 3,000 ton rake dashes by at an earth shaking velocity. No sooner has the southbound freight's swaying guards van passed from sight than a northbound freight goes through on the other side, the heavy throaty rhythm of the 'QJ' as it gathers speed through the station echoing and reverberating throughout the buildings.

But yet more is to come, for no sooner has the northbound passed than a heavy shunting movement struggles through the station. Tender first a 'JF' attempting to draw a mighty string of wagons from the yards, provides a superb performance despite, or, perhaps, because of her frenzied exhaust beats and occasional bouts of slipping! And so, within three minutes of our arrival at Siping we have seen four steam train movements. Before we leave a northbound express from Beijing to Harbin passes through at speed behind a diesel hydraulic and once the section is cleared we glide northwards again, all faces crammed to the windows on the west side of the train as we pass Siping shed, where at least twenty 'QJs' in full steam glisten in the sunlight.

We are travelling in open plan coaches, which are preferable for watching railway activities. The alternative compartment type double up as soft class sleepers at night. A round of light China tea is now enjoyed along with some cubes of Liu Dou Gau, a 'moreish' Chinese green bean cake. With Changchun now less than two hours away, we consider whether to have dinner on the train or in the hotel. Predictably the train finds favour and visits to the wash room provide the necessary freshening up prior to the meal. One forgets in the West how smutty and begrimed steam main line journeys can be! Despite the excellence of Chinese railways, no soap or towels, or even toilet paper are provided; experienced travellers carry these commodities amongst their hand luggage. Another piping hot dinner, suitably seasoned by the passing of a second 'Pacific', brings us to the outskirts of Changchun which is a kind of Chinese Crewe; a junction for several important routes and home of a huge locomotive works along with the rolling stock plant that builds 60 per cent of China Railways' coaching stock. Famed for its trams, film studios and automobile plant Changchun, 'the city

*On one of our visits to Changchun shed an 'SY' Class 2-8-2 added to the variety of locomotives present. She was however almost certainly an industrial engine which had called in for repairs on route to another destination.*

'of eternal spring', is one of the most important in China and has, through careful planning, retained a predominantly green appearance.

As we run through the suburbs, everyone lines the windows for passing the sheds on the left hand side. Alongside the allocation of 'QJs', 'JFs' and 'RMs' are a number of rare non-standard types. As our train draws to a halt the smiling face of our CITS guide, Mr Yen, appears alongside our carriage; he is standing in exactly the right position like the true professional that he is. He welcomes us to his city and quickly leads us through the thronged platforms to our waiting minibus and on to the magnificently appointed Changbiashan Guest House, one of Changchun's most prestigious tourist hotels. Our journey for the 189 miles (304 km) from Shenyang has taken 7 hours 5 minutes, an

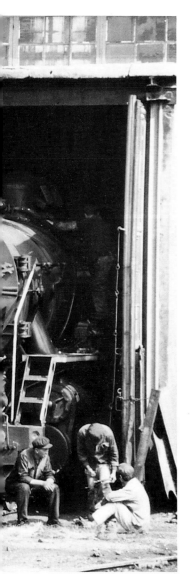

average of some 27 mph (43.5 kph). The best expresses over this section take some four hours, but there are no complaints for all agree that travelling such an exciting steam main line is one of the best ways of enjoying the railways of China and the landscape beyond. Over the seven-hour journey, our group calculate that we passed 25 southbound freights — almost one every quarter of an hour.

Changchun shed holds many delights, its allocation of 78 locomotives comprising fifty 'QJs', twenty 'JFs' and eight 'RMs'. However, these are augmented by examples of several classes lying derelict, especially distinctive amongst which a 'DB 1' 2-6-4, a typical American suburban passenger locomotive dating back to 1907, along with a 'DB 2' — a later Japanese-built version. Also present are Russian 'FD' 2-10-2s, a 'DK 1' 2-10-0, built in Japan for the South Manchurian Railway and an 'ST 3', one of eight massive 2-10-2s built in Belgium for the Lung Hai Railway. This awe-inspiring giant, with its massive grate area of 8.50 sq m (30.6 sq ft), is a perfect example of the kind of delights still to be found in China. Thus Changchun shed produces eight classes, representing locomotives built in five different countries.

Changchun's huge locomotive works are equally exciting. They were opened in 1958 and apart from building some of the early 'QJs', were responsible for re-gauging the Russian 'FDs'. Today, no building is undertaken, the shops serving as one of the major overhaul centres for China Railways, serving locomotives from the Changchun and Harbin areas.

The rolling stock works are nearby and in addition to building carriages for China Railways produces underground and metro stock, both for home and export. Opened during the 1950s, this vast complex comprises 27 separate shops, but in accordance with Changchun's character, the works contain a remarkable 140 varieties of trees and give the impression of a factory in a garden. Visiting it, I am reminded of a school trip to Cadbury's factory in Bournville, who actually used the term 'factory in a garden'. Over 8,000 workers are employed at the Changchun plant and British Rail Engineering Ltd have been in residence for some time, negotiating production of, and technical co-operation for BREL's International Coach.

Changchun is one of the busiest steam centres in China, and an amazing vantage point exists to the north of the station where the Harbin and Jilin lines diverge in the north-eastern suburbs of the city. This Chinese 'Clapham Junction' abounds in steam workings and if the 'JFs' on shunting and tripping movements are included, steam action occurs once every six minutes, including 'Pacifics' on both the Jilin and Harbin lines!

No visit to Changchun would be complete without an expedition on the city's tram network. This is China's most progressive tram system; it is built to standard gauge and operated by a hundred vehicles. Some examples date back to the 1940s but there are also modern 1980s-built units from Dalian. Changchun is one of four Chinese cities which retain trams, but the China Academy of Railway Sciences has expressed keen interest in extending this use of light rail, so eminently suitable

*Welding operations inside the smokebox of a 'JS' during re-assembly in the erecting shop at Changchun Locomotive Works.*

for the Chinese situation. Each year our 'Occidor' travel group hires a tram for a run across the system which culminates in a visit to the depot and workshops.

Changchun is but 150 miles (241.5 km) away from Harbin, gem of the north-east and the commercial and industrial capital of Heilongjiang Province. Harbin retains a friendliness guaranteed to captivate any visitor; it is also a magnificent railway centre upon which many lines converge, especially from the north and the city's huge marshalling yards form a clearing house for freight heading southwards through

*Derelict trams lie abandoned in their depot at Harbin. After being gradually cut-back over recent years, the final short stretch of line succumbed to buses in 1987.*

Manchuria, either to the port of Dalian, or onwards to Beijing and into the great China which lies beyond. Recent years have seen the dieselization of all passenger trains in the Harbin area, but virtually all freight remains steam.

'Sankong bridge in Harbin is the greatest train watching place in the world'. A modest structure with three arches, it overlooks the marshalling yards; one peep over the parapet rolls back the clock fifty years. Twelve steam locomotives may be visible scattered throughout the yard, their exhausts rising skywards amid a sea of wagons which stretch as

Harbin Tram Shed had a fine period atmosphere and would have made a fine backdrop for a scene from a Tennessee Williams play.

far as the eye can see. The bridge is located between two yards one of which makes up the formations for the northbound trains and the other those for southbound freights. Sankong bridge is actually built over the humping lines, with wagons rolling from the reception sidings to the south into the western part of Sankong yards for the northbound trains, whilst wagons rolling to the eastern part of the yard make up the formation for the southbound freights. The humping operations are fascinating, as wagons of many different types bearing every conceivable type of merchandise, roll in groups first through the king point then the queen points before crossing primary and secondary retarders — dramas set against the amplified voice of the yard controller as he directs operations. These shunting activities are interspersed with transfer freights and through freights, but the *'pièce de résistance'* is the majestic departure of the southbound freights, behind two 'QJs' or 'QJ' with 'JS' pilot, as they pass beneath the bridge to begin the assault on the climb up to Wang Gang.

Having watched the formation of the trains, the locomotives appear initially as specks in the distance on their way from the sheds. In the case of southbound departures, the light engines approach and pass under the bridge before reversing back into the yard to couple onto their trains. Pilot engines either follow or come in from the southside, having returned from taking a previous train up the bank.

On busy days it is no exaggeration to say that a steam locomotive passes every three minutes. This is certainly so when a 'JF' is humping for the southbound departures. The modest 'Mikado' makes a fine sight drawing 2,500 tons out of the yard. Slipping and occasionally stalling, she passes below watchers on the bridge with tortured exhaust beats shaking the structure in a distinctly alarming manner.

Harbin is known as 'China's coldest city', and in winter Sankong bridge must be the coldest spot in the country. The biting Manchurian wind blows across the yard from the north in vicious stinging blasts, and with daytime temperatures as low as minus 30 degrees centigrade it is difficult to remain there watching rail movements for any length of time. Yet the departing double-headers are without compare in such conditions, especially when seen against yards lightly dusted with snow. Once the two engines are in position, pressure is pumped into the Westinghouse system and plumes of steam rise into the sky. Almost simultaneously the mechanical stoker is put into operation, causing the white steam to turn myriad tones of grey. The head shunter appears with his flag and after a round of chime whistling, which rings out across the city, the cylinder cocks from first one and then the second locomotives burst into action, obliterating most of the backdrop. The colourful fronts of the engines become haloed in steam as the winter sun shines directly onto their dark boiler casings.

The first laboured exhaust beats send plumes of steam and smoke high into the air, where they remain miraculously preserved in the low temperature. The combination of steam spraying from the cylinder cocks, heavy throaty exhaust beats and musical chime whistles, pro-

*The view from Sankong bridge as a brace of 'QJ' Class 2-10-2s pulls heavily out of the yard with a southbound freight. The extreme right hand track is the humping line for the southbound yard, as witness the colour light, whilst the extensive yard for the northbound trains lies behind the engines' exhaust. Notice another double-headed freight is waiting to depart in the background.*

vides an audio-visual drama of the steam age without compare today. The trains begin to move out of the yard towards the bridge, each an explosion of sound and steam rolling down the track. Through the approaching circle of swirling steam a kaleidoscopic display of colours, slender fronts and silhouetted windshields bears down upon us.

As the giants pass beneath the bridge with their exhausts — occasionally in unison, but usually in rhythmic polyphony — striking the underside of the bridge, they envelop the road in a steamy fog, bringing all traffic to a halt. Should a shunting or a trip movement happen to occur at the same time, it can be over a minute before any activity can resume on the roadway. Sankong bridge not only provides some of the finest steam dramas left on earth, but it recalls the very essence of those childhood bridges in the halcyon days of great train watching, proving that the steam age in our home country was every bit as exciting as we remember it to have been.

During summer the pilot engines detach at Wang Gang station and return light to Harbin, but during the most severe part of the winter they continue with the train engine to Wujiatze. This is necessary because the grease in the axles throughout the train sets hard in the low temperatures and greatly increases the resistance, thus the pilot is needed until such time as the grease has softened sufficiently.

Away from the excitement of the railway and the marshalling yards Sankong's joys are enhanced by Harbin's unique 'Ice Festival', which takes place in the city's Zhaolin Park. The festival's central features are created by craftsmen using huge blocks of ice taken from the frozen Songhua river. The festival opens on 1 January and remains until the spring thaw in March. The exhibits range from animals, flowers and birds to replicas of palaces and churches, along with scenes from Chinese mythology, all carved to life-sized proportions. Each year's festival is different: the crowning glory of the 1987 exhibition was a towering replica of a Russian Orthodox church which stood in the centre of Harbin until it was pulled down by Mao's Red Guards during the Cultural Revolution. Each structure is festooned with light bulbs which, at night, render the festival a dazzling display of form and colour,

*Admission ticket to Harbin's Ice Festival in Zhaolin Park.*

哈尔滨冰灯游园会

THE HARBIN ICE—LANTERN GARDEN PARTY ICE LANTERNS

*A section of the 1985 travel group reposes on the east bank at Wang Gang summit during the morning session.*

through which the dark and heavily clad figures of visitors move in awe. A spectacular gateway of glittering ice twenty metres long and seven metres wide (65½ ft × 23 ft) forms the entrance to Zhaolin Park. Harbin's ice festival is, for me, the eighth wonder of the world and it attracts visitors from all over China.

Harbin's enchantment is all pervading, whether one stays at the International Hotel with its period 1930s' atmosphere or at the newer multi-storey luxury of the Swan Hotel. It matters little for in either case trains can be heard by night — when China's momentum quietens for a few hours — moving about their business in the yards. The sound of a distant steam train in the night is deeply reassuring; it adds a magic to the environment, like the howl of a wolf in Siberia, or the trumpeting of an elephant on African plains. Once such sounds are permitted to disappear the environment becomes impoverished.

Harbin in summer provides another major attraction for the 'Occidor' group, as the *finale* of our visit is to take a packed lunch for a day's action photography at the summit of Wang Gang bank. Our location lies in deep countryside at the end of a long straight section of line which passes through wooded cuttings. At 7.30 am having breakfasted early, the group assembles in the lobby in an atmosphere of almost childlike excitement, for many of our party will not have spent a day next to a busy steam main line for twenty years or more. The minibus

**Right** A 'JS' Class 2-8-2 races northwards past Saddle Mountain with a mixed freight.

**Bottom right** A 'QJ' Class 2-10-2 storms past our picnic spot at Wang Gang summit at the head of a Harbin to Changchun freight.

is piled high with photographic equipment, along with lunch boxes and flasks of boiling water for making the lineside coffee. As the autumn sunlight dispels the early mists, we head out into the countryside to the nearest point of road access to the summit. The minibus, along with our guide, returns to Wang Gang station where it will remain until we are ready to return. Our Chinese guide has been asked to brief the crews when the trains stop to release the pilot engine, to make some smoke for the British photographers waiting at the summit.

The rest of our journey to the vantage point is on foot and, heavily laden, we cross fields full of vegetables, aubergine, peppers, tomatoes, and cucumber all at the peak of ripeness. Their abundance is a reminder of the severe winter to come. It's 8.30 am: we will not rejoin the minibus until 5.00 pm, so we have eight clear hours next to the busiest steam-worked line in the world. There is a mystical air of anticipation. We do not know what the day will bring and dream of a photographic masterpiece — as elusive as a four-leaf clover. Reaching the railway we head southwards through the cutting and walk to the summit.

The line's direction is north to south, making the east bank perfect for morning photography and following a break when the sun is at its zenith, we cross to the west bank for the afternoon session.

Within minutes of our arrival a freight whistles its departure from Wang Gang station and tell-tale plumes of steam appear over the distant trees. Tripods are erected hurriedly and the bank zoned into photographic territory by the twenty members of our party. Meter readings are taken and exposure levels debated before the calling of complete silence in deference to those preparing sound recordings. The early morning air intensifies the sound of the approaching train working up towards us through the silent countryside. There is not a breath of wind and the temperature is too low for Wang Gang's chorus of field crickets to be in action. Then the labouring 'QJ' enters the cutting with a superb exhaust plume, the clean and well maintained engine sparkling in the early light. On every watching face there is a look of ecstasy for this is what we have come to see. As the tour leader this is all I could ever wish for, but on this occasion the enchantment is short lived. The piercing shriek of a northbound train takes us all by surprise as it races down the bank with an enormous rake of empties and before the guards van reaches us, the magnificent climbing train has steamed past in epic style, but the photographic composition has been spoilt by the train on the far line.

Soon the girls have the coffee stall-cum-picnic area set up beneath adjacent trees and lashings of Nescafé are dispensed, as the group commiserate over the lost picture. Coffee is barely finished before the cry goes up 'another one on the bank'. Again tripods are manned and we listen to the reverberating coughs of the toiling engine. This is not so inspiring, she is grimy, almost colourless and by the time she comes into the range of the cameras the exhaust has all but disappeared. As the daytime temperature increases exhaust effects would become ever more fickle.

A 'JS' Class 2-8-2, banked by a 'QJ', climbs away from Nancha with the 07.25 passenger train to Yichun.

**Above right** With cylinder cocks open and mechanical stoker activated a 'JS' struggles to start a southbound freight from Sankong yard in a temperature of minus 30° centigrade.

**Far right** 'QJ' Class 2-10-2 No 290 acting as pilot to a sister engine also struggles to start its train from Sankong yard amid the depths of the Manchurian winter.

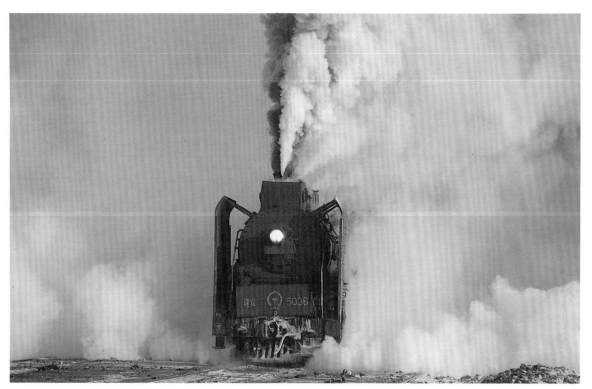

The sleek streamlined form of preserved 'SL7' Class 'Pacific' No 751 — one of the few locomotives restored to working order by the Railway Museum in Shenyang.

By the end of the morning session at 11.30 three more freights have climbed the bank, one hauled by an immaculate 'QJ' with superb exhaust effect whilst another had a 'JS' as pilot. Eight freights have passed heading north, all making a fine spectacle as the 'QJs' dash down the bank at up to 50 mph, some oscillating quite alarmingly. Most of the northbound trains blew down at the top of the summit ejecting the scum from the bottom of the boiler into the atmosphere. This was obviously a designated point for this activity. After twelve trains and with at least a couple of superb pictures in the bag, lunch is called.

With the sun now almost overhead, the wheels of the locomotive are in inky shadow as they pass. Afternoon photography does not begin in earnest until 2 o'clock on the opposite side of the bank.

Another round of coffee is brewed and lunch packs opened, as we begin our picnic in the tranquillity of the lush Chinese country-side, amid banks laced with wild flowers and bedecked with butter-flies. A pair of hawks circle effortlessly overhead, a warbler sings a scratchy song from a lineside bush and crickets and grasshoppers churr away in unison. The soft drone of a 'DFH 3' diesel can be heard ascending the bank and we calculate that this must be the thrice-weekly express from Moscow to Beijing via Harbin.

Shortly after 1 o'clock we see a 'QJ' climbing the bank with what looks like a huge headlamp blazing from its smokebox. 'It's *Zhou De*' I shout, No 2470, the pride of Harbin and the most magnificently kept locomotive on China Railways. The headlamp is actually the golden face of General 'Zhou De', staring impassively outwards from a large brass plate on the locomotive's smokebox.

'Zhou De' was one of China's ten great marshals and the man who led the Red Army from its formation in 1927, through the revolution of 1949 when he was second only to Mao himself; indeed before 1949, the Red Army was known as the Zhou De-Mao Army. What a shame, that this magnificent engine, with its gleaming brass work and superb-ly polished trims should pass at high sun when conditions for photo-graphy are at their worst.

What will happen during the afternoon session? The unpredict-able dominates every moment, just as it does in fine sport, for the best pictures often come from lucky breaks; a twist of smoke, a colourful engine, the right length of train, the right type of wagons combined with that indefinable quirk of camera position, focal length of lens and precise aperture. During these days at Wang Gang I think of cricket, for as the hours roll by we wait — like the cricketer — for that 'lucky ball' which transforms the day.

During the afternoon two diesel-hauled expresses climb the bank and thereby reduce the steam activity until close of play at 4.30. The afternoon session is even more tense than the morning's, for as the shadows lengthen, China's late September light turns to a liquid gold and shadows from the lineside conifers creep progressively down the embankment. These provide a superb contrast during the mid-after-noon, but by 4 o'clock they touch onto the northbound line and by

*'QJ' Class 2-10-2 No 2470 Zhou De approaches the summit at Wang Gang with a southbound freight from Harbin. This study was made in afternoon sunlight from the west bank.*

4.30 pm are lapping up against the wheels of the southbound trains. My ambition at this location is to photograph *Zhou De* climbing the bank emitting a column of grey exhaust skywards and with her half-mile-long train tailing back through the cutting to a breathtakingly distant infinity. This would be the 'ball' which tips the balance of the game and provides the one masterpiece which sends the photographer away from the lineside bathed in a glow of enchantment; exactly, I suspect, as a cricketer might feel having scored a mighty six that takes him over the century.

At 3.10 pm we score that century! A freight train goes down the bank complete with an ex-works 'JS', towed tender first within the rake, on route to its home depot and no sooner has this train passed than a climbing freight rounds the distant bend. As the resplendent 'QJ' approches the camera, the mechanical stoker is activated — almost certainly in response to our guide's request — the exhaust darkens dramatically and the magnificent 2-10-2 with bright red driving wheels, blue front and glistening brass boiler bands, looms into the viewfinder. Shutters fire, power winders whirr and shouts of elation rise up as the crew wave an acknowledgement, despite being visibly over-awed by the jubilation on the bank! This is the picture of the day, the perfect lineside action shot of a big locomotive performing at its best in perfect light!

Throughout the day we cannot help but be aware of the privileged position we are in: we compare our fortunate lot with that of the line-side photographer in Europe waiting for one preserved steam rail tour to pass, with all the vagaries of lighting and circumstance which invariably conspire to spoil his picture. We can afford to let a train pass if the engine is too dirty, or not showing sufficient exhaust. We have the same advantages as lineside photographers from the golden years of steam, for they were able to sit at the trackside in contemplative leisure and take only the scenes which inspired them most.

*Detail study of 'QJ' Class 2-10-2 No 2470 Zhou De — the pride of Harbin.*

*A 'QJ' Class 2-10-2 smokily labours its way through the cuttings on the approach to Wang Gang summit at the head of a Harbin to Changchun freight.*

Our day of 'cricket in the sun' is over: it is close of play, 4.30 pm, the picnic is packed away whilst mounds of photographic and recording equipment, which have littered the banks are returned to their cases. For some of the group it will be their last day on a busy steam main line; most may never get back to China, but this incredible experience, will provide an enduring memory. Such are our thoughts as, in file, we trudge back across the fields. In eight hours at the lineside we have seen twelve steam trains climbing the bank and fourteen heading down, 26 in all, or an average of one every eighteen minutes. But our great day is not over yet, for as we return to Harbin, bound for the Swan Hotel, thoughts turn to the banquet awaiting us that evening. On our final day in Harbin it has become a tradition for our group to be given a banquet by our friends in the China travel service.

A good Chinese banquet is an experience to be savoured for it produces the most exotic food on earth in the most convivial of circumstances. Along with our Chinese friends we sit around an enormous table with a revolving centre to enable everyone easy access to the dishes. Drinks include local beer, orange juice, wines and spirits for the many toasts. The meal is served leisurely and lasts several hours, each round of dishes being freshly prepared and brought at intervals. We begin with *hors d'oeuvre* consisting of nuts, spiced vegetables, soya strips and cold chicken, after which come the first hot dishes: pork in beansprouts, shrimps in onion and vegetable and roast beef chunks. Before this is eaten the toasts begin: everyone at the table being expected to propose as and when he pleases. Toasts in Harbin are normally drunk from a small glass of white spirit and if the proposer calls '*Gambey*' it indicates that the entire glass of spirit has to be downed in one. After a few '*Gambeys*', the mood at table becomes livelier than ever. Conversation flows and the repast before us becomes yet more enjoyable. China's rich gastronomic traditions are handed down from its feudal past and one of the many miracles of the 1949 revolution is the availability of such occasions to the proletariat — albeit to the management and professional grades.

Now a break for those who smoke: huge dragon's head ashtrays are provided and the small glasses constantly topped with spirit. At one point Mr Lou Binsheng, manager of CITS, Harbin, rises to his feet to propose a toast and raising his glass solemnly declares, 'To the year 1804'. Everyone looks bemused until I suddenly realize what he means: on my previous visit I told him that the world's first steam locomotive ran in that year.

Then the table is enlivened with pork in batter — both sweet and sour and pancakes, to be self-rolled, with meat sauce and fresh celery, but the pride of the table is the 'Lion's Head', an enormous casserole in an earthenware dish. Another break until the following round comes; scrambled eggs with prawns and the first soup in the form of a pasta noodle. Now the '*Gambeys*' come thick and fast helped along with hot meat dumplings dipped in red soya sauce. A good banquet, like an orchestral symphony, moves ever towards a resounding climax.

And so to bed, to muse on exotic feasts, laced with the smoke, the smell of the grass, the sound of the trains, and the endless rolling freights. All combine to engender a deep feeling of peace conducive to the finest of slumbers.

# Chapter 4

# Steam and coal

Coal provides much of China's energy but reserves are often far from industrial centres. The country's rapid expansion over recent years has caused serious transportation difficulties. Shanghai, China's largest industrial base, produces one sixth of the national annual revenue, but all the area's coal comes either from the northern or eastern parts of the country. Shortages often occur and yet in Shanxi province, China's largest coal base, millions of tons lie on the ground awaiting transport, with losses caused by spontaneous combustion, rain and exposure.

Coal is also a key export commodity for vital foreign exchange. China has an estimated reserve of some two thousand billion tons, with known reserves of six hundred billion. So vast is the potential, that if Shanxi doubled its current output from just known reserves, it could continue production for 800 years! With coal available in such plenty and an abundance of labour in a controlled market economy, it is little wonder that steam traction has survived, especially in the coal producing regions of Shanxi and the North East. But the scope for development today is so rapid that China regards electrified routes as being the only possible way of moving the necessary tonnage from the coalfield to the eastern and southern parts of the country and to the eastern coastal ports for export. At present coal accounts for well over 50 per cent of the freight on China's five major rail trunk lines: Beijing-Guangzhou, Beijing-Shanghai, Lanzhou-Lianyungang, Beijing-Shenyang and Harbin-Dalian.

A number of exciting new railways are being constructed to solve the problem along with electrification of existing lines — notably that from Datong to Beijing which until electrification some years ago saw a steam hauled train with a 2,500 ton load leave Shanxi every ten minutes. In the near future, two new electrified trunk lines running east to west will take Shanxi's coal to the sea, the most famous is the Daqin line from Datong to Quinhuagdao whilst the other route further south will run from Houma to Shijiusuo. The Daqin line is intended to be fully operational by 1991 and 6,000 ton trains comprised of seventy-ton bogie wagons are envisaged, with an intention to operate 10,000 ton trains in the longer term — the line's ultimate capacity being put at one hundred million tons a year. Sidings a mile in length are being planned to permit such massive trains.

In the longer term then it is electrified main lines rather than steam-operated ones that will be moving China's coal, but it will be many years yet before the 'QJs' are displaced from long distance coal hauls and even when they are, many secondary and feeder lines will continue to be worked economically by steam. Furthermore, it is probable that new designs of steam locomotives may yet appear (a theme I explore in a later chapter).

China's traditional coal capital is Fushun, which lies some 25 miles to the east of Shenyang in Liaoning Province. Fushun's huge western open cast mine produces twelve million tons of oil shale (7 per cent oil) and five million tons of coal a year. The town has three iron and steel works and three oil refineries, handling both shale and crude, piped in from oilfields lying to the north of Harbin. Also in evidence is an enormous thermal power station. The north bank of the western open cast has a belt of heavy industries related to it, which spew smoke and steam all over the town. In the winter the haze rarely clears before mid-morning. All this heavy industrial endeavour is set amid a tapestry of Dickensian dwellings, small, cramped and reached by long back alleys, which provide common access.

The Fushun Mining Administraton's railway is largely electrified, although a little steam traction is used and two of the classes are of immense historical importance in locomotive evolution. One is the former China Railway's 'KD6' Class, 2-8-0s which are examples of the celebrated United States Army Transportation Corps 'S160s'. The other type are the ex-China Railway's 'DK5' 2-10-0s, which were built in Rumania by Resita. These, in fact, are Rumanian copies of the German Class '50' of 1938. The '50s' formed one of the world's classic types. Along with their wartime relations the '*Kriegslokomotive*', they numbered some 10,000 examples and both versions survive active in Eastern Europe to this day. On my first visit to Fushun in 1984, I was lucky to achieve a picture of a 'KD6' with a 'DK5' behind, both boiling up in the depot yard; a theme which depicted American and German World War 2 locomotives side by side some forty years later.

Also on the Mining Authority's metals was an original 'JF' 'Mikado', one of the first examples from Alco as supplied to the South Manchurian Railway in 1918. All three of these Fushun classes were built in their thousands and, if variations are taken into account they total, between them, over 15,000 locomotives. This is a marvellous example of the fascinating non-standard types which can still be found in China, particularly in coalfield service, although sadly, such rarities are rapidly being phased out.

My most exciting coalfield experience in China was a visit to Manzhouli on the Russian border, at the height of winter in February 1987. This trip was the result of a long-standing ambition sparked off by Mr

*'KD6' Class No 478 in action on the metals of the Fushun Mining Administration with a Rumanian built 'DK5' Class 2-10-2 in the background. 'KD6' 478 was a member of the famous U.S.A.T.C. 'S160' Class was built by Lima of Ohio, as their works number 8270 in May 1943.*

Jang of CITS Harbin, who had frequently mentioned the varied steam types to be found there. So it was, that we left the Swan Hotel on a bitter winter's night to catch the 21.50 sleeping car train for the 19½-hour journey from Harbin to Manzhouli. We travelled soft sleeper and as usual, upon entering our compartment, flasks of boiling water were provided. We were asked if we would like dinner, the restaurant car still being in full operation: the train was warm and comfortable despite the outside temperature being a frightening minus forty degrees centigrade.

Upon waking at 9 o'clock the next morning, our train was heading through the Inner Mongolian hills, which gave way progressively to vast grassy plains. It was a wonderful feeling to be travelling this historical route, which was once the principal way of travelling from Europe to Peking. I thought of the luxury expresses in all their elegance which plied this route in the pre-aviation age.

Eventually the diesel belt was left behind and an 'SL6' 'Pacific' headed our train. She made superb progress over the single track route and was every bit as fast as our earlier diesel had been. It was a glorious experience, to sit in comfort, listening to the chime whistle of an 'SL6' echoing across the plains and to watch the endless trails of fluffy white smoke drifting past the carriage windows. In a watery, winter sun we rolled across the grasslands on the approach to Hailaer.

Hailaer is an important industrial town with huge sidings in which long formations of coal, wood and oil trains stand, waiting for the southward journey. The huge steam shed held 'QJ's, 'JFs' and 'Pacifics'. Late in the afternoon we reached Yakoshih, another important industrial centre where belching chimneys and gaunt Russian-style factories provided a setting that would have inspired Lowry. Dark huddled figures moved against this backdrop along streets covered with snow. The colour tones accentuated by the weak sunlight produced an effect very reminiscent of a traditional Lowry landscape and it was a strange feeling to experience such scenes of Lancashire and an earlier industrial Britain in the unlikely setting of a small town in Inner Mongolia.

Here we had a chance to examine our locomotive, located fourteen coaches away at the head of the train. It was 'SL6' 'Pacific' No 691, a Sifang engine built during the 1950s. We had passed many collieries throughout the day, but reaching Zalainoer we glimpsed a huge complex which was obviously the coal-working area for Manzhouli and another 12½ miles (20 km) through a Patagonian type landscape brought us to the huge modern station.

Manzhouli is in China's Inner Mongolia autonomous region, and the station is just a few kilometres from the Soviet border. A bitter wind was blowing in from Siberia as we paid our respects to the Pacific before she un-coupled to go to the shed. It is here that through trains to Moscow give way to a Soviet diesel which takes the coaches forward to the border, where the wheels are changed from China's stan-

*Destination boards on the coaches of the overnight passenger train from Harbin to Manzhouli.*

dard to Russia's 5ft gauge. Manzhouli's huge marshalling yards handle half of all the Sino-Soviet rail freight which totals some three million tons each year.

Next morning, whilst arrangements were being made for us to go to the colliery we took an opportunity to see the town. The streets were wide and clean and there was a tremendous air of prosperity: wherever we looked construction work was taking place. Many of the old Soviet style homes had been renovated, including the Sino-Soviet friendship building. The town has many industries, including a fine carpet factory, a brewery, a dried milk plant, fish farms, a canning factory and, despite the short summer season, considerable agriculture. We learned that 43 kilometres away was the vast Hulun Lake covering 2,300 sq km. This paradise on earth has 31 species of indigenous fish whilst no less than 240 species of bird have been recorded in the area, including swans, geese, ducks, eagles, cranes and gulls.

On our arrival at the colliery, we were introduced to the chief engineer, Mr Lieu, and enquired exactly what type of locomotives they had. He produced a roster book which appeared to detail every locomotive that had ever worked there. The list was impressive, 'SY' and 'JS' 'Mikados', 'KD6' ('S160') and 'KD2' 2-8-0s, 'QJ' 2-10-2s and 'SK' Class number B101, which turned out to be a derelict American 0-4-0 Saddle Tank, complete with wooden buffer beam. Presumably she had been delivered for the colliery's opening in 1902, when coal production was largely earmarked to supply fuel for the newly-opened East China Railway.

Mr Lieu explained that two of the four 'KD6s' were working and two were now out of use. All the 'KD2s' it seems were condemned. This later type came from Xian in 1978 when the colliery bought them direct from China Railways. Typically French in appearance, they resembled the SNCF '140C' Class of World War 1 origin. These 'KD2s' were built in Belgium for the former Lung-Hai Railway, an east-west trunk route across central China which linked Gansou, Shaanxi, Henan and Jiangsu provinces with the sea. Apparently the type had not found favour in Zalainoer and had only seen one year's service in the colliery.

The most active engines were the 'SY' 'Mikado' Class locomotives with 35 in service. The 'SYs' are a medium-sized engine for industrial use: all have been built at Tangshan where, as we shall see, production continues today. Capable engines of extremely handsome proportions, the 'SYs' see service throughout Chinese industry, particularly collieries but also in other mines, factories, steel works etc. With 20.8 in (52.8 cm) diameter cylinders and a tractive effort of over 38,000 lb, the 'SYs' prove ideal for heavy industrial hauls where sustained capacity over relatively long distances is necessary. We were surprised to find two 'JSs' on Zalainoer's list and this was an interesting example of downgrading since these engines are almost exclusively found in main line service. Even more remarkable was the fact that the list also included five 'QJs'. These had been delivered in 1979 from Fengtai yards in Beijing by special concession — presumably when Fengtai's operations were dieselized. Apparently Zalainoer urgently needed locomotives and the Tangshan earthquake, having stopped production of 'SYs', caused 'QJs' to be drafted in as an emergency measure. A painting in the General Manager's Office clearly depicted them working on the terraces deep inside the open-cast mines.

Complete standardization to 'SYs' was envisaged as soon as new locomotives could be obtained from Tangshan: only recently three other non-standard types had vanished from Zalainoer; 'PL 21' 2-6-2Ts from Orenstein and Koppel, 'JF5' 'Mikados' and 'SL3' 'Pacifics'. We were told

*Former China Railways' 'JF6' Class No 3154 enjoys a further lease of life in coalfield service at Zalainoer.*

*Part of Zalainoer's vast open cast coal mine, depicting the exhausts of five different steam trains. Notice the terracing and the way in which the trains zig-zag their way down to the various levels.*

that the Wild Goose colliery at Hailaer which we had intended to visit, as a potential source of rarities, was now entirely worked by 'SYs'.

Although Manzhouli has several slope mines, it is the vast open-cast pit which forms the principal activity; the lines zig-zag down to a depth of 260 ft (80 m) along terraces some 30 ft (10 m) in depth, the out-cropping coal being clearly visible. Loaded trains leave the pit with either spoil or coal, the latter being graded in the nearby washery before being taken to the connection sidings with the main line.

Most of Zalainoer's coal is used regionally, half going to electricity generating plants and some to iron and steel plants in the vicinity and the rest for local domestic consumption. Any surpluses are sent to Harbin. The open cast is worked exclusively by 'SYs' with older 'Mikados' and the 'KD6s' being used on shunting and engineers' service trains. The activity we saw was incredible, with loading being undertaken from several terraces throughout the pit. The exhausts of up to a dozen locomotives could be seen in various modes of operation, whilst the double track route which led into the pit, over which empties and loaded trains passed, added further excitement with trains going by every few minutes. Operations at Zalainoer come under the North-East Coal Administration Bureau. There are seven collieries within this enterprise in Inner Mongolia and Zalainoer is the third largest.

One of our main priorities was to find a 'KD6', and we finally ran one to ground hauling an engineers' track-laying train, which slewed the rails in accordance with the advancement of the mining operation. We travelled with this train in order to take pictures as the operations were being carried out, but the bitter wind made photography extremely difficult: it attacked out faces like a carving knife, whilst the necessity to wear several layers of gloves made the cameras difficult to operate. To remove one's gloves, even for a minute, was to invite agony afterwards, necessitating minutes of pumping arms and fingers in a desperate bid to restore circulation. The wind also caused constantly running eyes, which not only made focussing difficult, but on occasions, actually froze eyelashes to camera. Had we not had access to the warmth of the 'KD6' cab, photographic work would have been almost impossible. In such conditions one's resistance rapidly declines and concentration ebbs at an alarming rate. With our breath freezing onto our scarves in icy needles and with our camera straps frozen into bent unwieldy forms, we persevered, for time with so rare a design was short and our quarry had been elusive. The photographic day had finished by three in the afternoon, since by this time the sun was too weak for effective work.

But such discomforts are irrelevant compared with the important task of documenting this classic war locomotive. The most numerous wartime class produced from the United States, some 2,120 locomotives appeared from Baldwin and Lima between 1942 and 1945. Built to the British loading gauge, they first arrived in 1942 and hundreds of them saw service in Britain before following the Allied Armies in the advance across Europe. As a result of wartime operation and subsequent post-war dispersal, 'S160s' appeared in many countries but these examples relegated to coalfield service in China form some of the last active examples in the world.

After an action-packed day, we rejoined our vehicle and headed back across the grassland to Manzhouli, with the main line several hundred metres to the west. The sun had almost set and the snow reflected its golden haze under the deepest of blue skies. Surveying the wild expanse, I tried to imagine summer and the flocks of wild geese which would return to these vast breeding grounds. Glancing casually behind, my heart missed a beat, for overtaking us was the evening passenger train from Harbin with a gleaming 'SL6' at the head of seventeen coaches. As the train drew level the 'Pacific' became silhouetted against the declining sun. An orange reflection danced in the cab and a glorious white smoke trail rose high above the coaches and, echoing the curvature of the line, extended back for a distance of several clear miles across the evening grassland.

One by one the illuminated coaches of the train overtook us until the whole formation was visible ahead. Here in the wilderness of Inner Mongolia the poignant beauty of the steam train re-asserted itself: the scene was so beautiful, so removed from reality as to seem as if seen through the innocent eyes of a child. We watched it disappear in sheer wonder, until only the red tail lamp and orange fire reflection in the

An 'SY' Class 'Mikado' waits in the open cast mine at Zalainoer for the digger to fill the wagons with coal. The factory chimney in the far distance is next to the washery at the top of the open cast.

*'KD6' Class No 482 was one of Zalainoer's two working examples of this type. Notice how the appearance of these classic American war veterans has been altered by the fitting of a taller chimney for improved drafting.*

dancing steam were discernible, before they too finally disappeared into a rapidly advancing twilight.

The warmth and comfort of our hotel made up for the cold and tribulations of the bitter winter that we had suffered all day. By 8 o'clock I fell asleep naturally, not through tiredness, but with a sensation similar to that induced after drinking a heavy wine on a hot summer day. The slumber so produced lasts for eight or more hours, by which time one is well prepared to meet the challenges of another day.

# Chapter 5

# Steam and steel

When I first heard about Anshan Iron and Steel works, I could scarcely believe that such a place existed. Countless blast furnaces in all their fiery glory formed a centrepiece of a vast industrial complex into which iron ore is brought from vast mines in the neighbouring countryside. And the whole place is alive with steam locomotives: dozens of them, embracing many different classes. It all seemed too good to be true, even in China, for it sounded like the kind of complex which mushroomed during the 19th century at the height of the industrial revolution.

With great anticipation then I boarded a Dalian-bound express in Shenyang for the 89-kilometre run to Anshan in January 1984. The Shenyang to Dalian line is one of the busiest in China and sees heavy steam traffic. After passing the marshalling yards and depot at Sujatun we continued past many industrial complexes interspersed with open stretches of rolling agricultural land. Long before reaching Anshan, I realized the truth of the tales for on the west side of the line, after passing extensive interchange sidings the industrial complex appeared, becoming increasingly dense and overpowering, until nothing could be seen behind the enormous structures which bordered the main line.

I was met on the platform by Zhou Yongli who cordially announced that I was the second English visitor to arrive within a few days, as my visit followed that of David Blunkett and his Sheffield city councillors, who had visited Anshan to twin the two cities. Zhou had guided the party and spoke well of Sheffield's blind leader, his good humour and intellect and of the economic and cultural links they hoped to forge. I remember the thrill I felt on hearing of this association — the first Anglo-Sino twinning — nowhere on earth could be more appropriate for Anshan to be associated with and I thought of the days when Sheffield was at its industrial height and known as 'hell with the lid off'. Perhaps it would have resembled the Anshan of today. I preferred not to tell my Chinese friends that much of Sheffield's heavy industry had now been closed down, that many

**Above** *An Anshan Mining Administration electric locomotive at the base of the huge Dagushan open cast mine to the south of the city.*

collieries, foundries and factories were running at a low key and that the area suffered from a high rate of unemployment, though I suspected that they knew. That first visit to Anshan was the first of many, Zhou was to become a close friend and I came to love the city. The ever-welcoming Anshan Guest House was to become a kind of second home.

Anshan means 'Saddle Mountain', the name being taken from two such mountains to the south of the city, one of which has since disappeared as a result of the mining. The area is surrounded by rich deposits of iron ore and primitive methods of smelting were undertaken here before the birth of Christ. Today however, the ore from these outlying areas is conveyed to the complex by the Anshan Mining Company's

electrified railway. This network begins from a separate station in Anshan and runs south roughly parallel with the Dalian line for a mile or so before crossing it and gradually working its way back to cross it again several miles to the north of Anshan, so forming a kind of circle. There are sixteen stations on this route and innumerable branches lead to the various mines. A passenger service also operates, primarily for the needs of workers as the entire operation at Anshan employs over 250,000 people.

It was a fascinating and unusual discovery to find that the mining branches were electrified while the main line of China Railways was steam operated and doubly interesting to find out that the electric locomotives were older than the steamers on the main line! Electric railways in China began as early as 1914 for the local operations at Fushun, which were then under the control of the South Manchurian Railway. Anshan's 1,500 volt DC system has a fascinating variety of locomotives, of Japanese, Czechoslovakian and German as well as indigenous Chinese origin.

Production from the Anshan industrial complex is an unbelievable 13.85 million tons of iron and steel a year and the activity necessary to produce this total has to be seen to be believed. Sixty different factories make up the site, including ten blast furnaces, three steel mills, a sinter plant, a huge coking plant, twenty rolling mills, two power stations, a refactory and machine repair shops. Ninety per cent of the iron ore is locally mined: the missing ten per cent being of a different grade for making specific types of steel and this is brought in by main line railway.

China Railways bring in phenomenal tonnages of other commodities too; coal — primarily from Fushun — along with scrap metal, limestone, and magnesium in addition to the materials necessary to keep the complex in good repair and in a constant state of development — 17½ million tons of iron and steel is the targeted production for 1990!

Anshan's output includes cast iron, steel billets, shaped steel, steel sheets and strips, girders, rails, tubes and wires. Some items go directly to Dalian for export but most are for domestic use, including pig iron and steel for the steam locomotive works in Datong in Inner Mongo-

**Right** *Anshan's operations are eloquently mirrored on the Five Yuan bank note. The upper side depicts a foundry worker, whilst on the rear, an electrically-hauled ironstone train passes between two mechanical diggers with a steam train seen halfway up the open cast in the far distance.*

lia. Processed slag is another bulk commodity which is despatched to factories throughout China for cement and brick production, although the complex also manufactures some cement of its own.

Each visitor to Anshan will have his favourite amongst its multifarious activities; for me there are many high spots. Most impressive, perhaps, is Steel Mill No 1, with its bank of open hearth furnaces in full cry. These look like a scene from an early 19th century oil painting depicting the birth of the industrial revolution. Mechanical feeders

**Right and above right** 'YJ' *Class 'Prairie' No 288, takes a breather in front of Blast Furnace number 7 during workaday chores at Anshan Iron & Steel Works.*

add the additional elements to the iron to make the steel which then passes to huge ladle wagons waiting below, before transfer to the Rough Rolling Mill.

Another favourite activity is watching the blast furnaces fill the cauldron wagons with molten iron or slag. Most of the slag is now tipped into water, in order to bring about the chemical change which renders it suitable for cement manufacture. As the liquid slag hits the liquid a cloud of steam rises skywards like an atomic explosion, utterly dwarfing the vociferous excrements of the coke ovens and power stations. Surplus slag is tipped in the traditional manner down the slag bank and watching these activities is to witness an archaic industrial drama now on the verge of extinction.

The railway network reaches every nook and cranny of the complex, with steam, diesel and electric locomotives in use. There are fifteen 'main lines' from which the branches diverge and the complex is divided into twelve railway control areas, each locomotive being allocated to one of these zones. Engines are serviced within the complex and only return to the main locomotive works when in need of major repair. The motive power roster includes 188 locomotives but not all are in use, the active total embraces approximately fifty electrics, forty steam and twenty diesels.

'Mikados' and 'Prairies' predominate amongst the steam locomotives, the former being either 'JF6', 'SY' or 'JSs' while the latter group is made up of 'PL2s' and 'YJs' — two classes not frequently seen elsewhere. Both are industrial designs and are regarded as smaller versions of the 'JF6'. The 'PL2s' are older, having originated in Japan in the 1940s, whereas the 'YJ' is exclusively Chinese-built from the 1960s. These are all large locomotives and they follow American traditions — Anshan's roster reflecting the kind of motive power one might have found at a similar complex in America half a century ago.

A few small engines exist in the 'XK' series, by far the most notable being the five 'XK2s', another famous American design from World War 2. These locomotives were designed for the United States Army Transportation Corps as the standard shunter for Allied operations in Europe. These — like the 'S1 60s' — saw service in many countries. They first appeared in 1942 and over 500 were built by H.K. Porter, Vulcan of Wilks Barr and Davenports of Ohio. They saw wartime service in Western Europe, Greece, the Middle East and North Africa. When hostilities ceased, they became surplus to military requirements and America's railways had no use for them. As new utility shunting engines,

*One of Anshan Iron & Steel Works' 'XK2' Class 0-6-0Ts. Several of these American war veterans remain active within the complex and are retained for working in restricted confines where clearances are severely limited.*

however, the type found favour in civilian use in many parts of the globe.

Sadly the number of diesels is increasing, primarily because they enable the steam servicing points to be removed, thus saving both space and manpower. The works' management seem keen to utilize every tiny parcel of land in this burgeoning complex. Steam locomotives need to be coaled and watered regularly and this takes up valuable time, also coal trains moving around the complex delivering fuel to the various servicing areas are seen to clog up the system. Manpower saved on steam traction could be used productively elsewhere, for in socialist China unemployment, as known to us in the West, does not exist. These sen-

*'YJ' Class Industrial Prairie No 290 threads its smoky way between the blast furnaces at Anshan Iron & Steel Works.*

'Industrial Shepherd'; one of
Anshan Iron & Steel Works'
smut-covered white-eyed men,
having just released molten slag
from Blast Furnace number 9.

**Above right** One of Anshan
Iron & Steel Works' former US
Army 'XK2' Class 0-6-0Ts
prepares to draw ladles out of
Steel Mill number 3.

**Right** Sections of an 'SY'
locomotive's bar frames being
trimmed in the casting shop at
Tangshan. Notice the rough cast
driving wheel in the lower right
foreground.

*Cauldrons being filled with molten slag below Blast Furnace number 9 in Anshan Iron & Steel Works.*

**Above right** *An 'SY' Class 2-8-2 on slag tipping duties at Anshan Iron & Steel Works.*

**Below right** *Cauldrons of liquid slag being emptied at Anshan Iron & Steel Works.*

'YJ' Class Industrial 'Prairie' No 290 waits to draw ladles of molten iron away from Blast Furnace number 2 at Anshan Iron & Steel Works.

timents underline the unstoppable nature of the Chinese people in industrial endeavours. As a nation they seem to possess a singleness of purpose and an ability to think in straight lines, with a determination to eradicate any inefficiencies which stand in their way.

Another factor against the use of steam traction is pollution. The whole complex is responsible for appalling emissions, which, under adverse atmospheric conditions, can choke the town in an industrial haze and deposit a residue of grime over the countryside for miles around. Considerable progress has been made towards reducing the worst emissions, but unfortunately the steam locomotive, though it causes only a small part of the problem, receives a disproportionate amount of blame from emotive campaigners. However, the Chinese readily accept that the relative cheapness of steam locomotives combined with their simplicity and dependence on locally mined fuel, are factors in their favour and the complex continually presses the Railway Ministry for new 'SYs'. These engines are primarily to replace older 'Mikados' acquired from the national railway system, but some are also needed to cope with the rapid actual and projected increase in output.

Future intentions are to reduce the railway operation in certain areas by using huge conveyor belt systems, although longer term developments are likely to incorporate the siting of related plants adjacent to one another so dispensing with the need for rail operation between them.

Further railway interest in Anshan is provided by the city's tramway network, which consists of a single 600v DC route 8 miles (13 km) long. The system dates back to the 1950s and a fleet of 77 cars provides services to the steel complex. Included are a number of new cars delivered from Dalian in 1983 to replace older Japanese-built examples acquired secondhand from Shenyang when that city abandoned its trams in 1978. The system runs past the Anshan Guest House and the pleasant evenings to be enjoyed there include watching the trams rattle by. At night their blue electric flashes periodically illuminate the bedrooms — a drama enhanced by the sound of steam trains on the main line and the reverberating roar of charges to the blast furnaces.

Our 'Occidor' travel group visits to Anshan always include a lineside stint near Saddle Mountain, for the 397-kilometre line from Shenyang to Dalian was, until recently, the busiest steam line in China carrying enormous quantities of coal, oil and timber bound for export. Apart from 'QJs' the line also sees 'JS' Class locomotives on freights along with 'SL6' Class 'Pacifics' on stopping passenger services — three being seen on an average morning session. Our location overlooks the remaining half of Saddle Mountain, which looms up behind the northbound trains as they round the bend and approach over a long stretch of straight track. It is a superb viewpoint and the morning sun is perfect: the complex is visible to the north, while to the east, the Mining Administration's electric trains can be seen at work. However, upon making our usual foray in September 1987, we found that some 30 per cent of the trains were operated by new diesels imported from General

*An impressive line-up of electric locomotives belonging to the Anshan Mining Administration at their depot near the east gate of the complex. The three engines in the centre are Bo Bo Bo's built in East Germany for the complex's 1,500v DC system.*

*Above The 'SL6' 'Pacifics' form adds a touch of distinction to the Shenyang to Dalian main line. Here one passes our lineside location near Saddle Mountain at the head of a northbound stopping train.*

*Left A smoky drama within the main sheds of the Anshan Iron & Steel complex, depicting two 'SY' Class 2-8-2s.*

Electric in the USA. The stream of 'QJs', 'JSs' and 'Pacifics' rendered the morning worthwhile, but the occasion served as a serious reminder that even in China diesels can encroach at short notice and if any more are drafted this celebrated line will lose its preferred status amongst visiting groups more appreciative of steam-hauled trains.

Never to my dying day will I forget a session on that line with Zhou in January 1984. He had taken me to another location on the opposite side of Saddle Mountain where the morning sun favoured the south-bound trains. Two minutes after our arrival a 'QJ' passed at the head of a 3,000 ton haul and before the train had disappeared a second pall of steam was visible in the distance and behind that a third one. This was repeated until eight trains had passed southwards — one every 5½ minutes. They were literally leaving Anshan one behind the other, 'QJ' or 'JS' hauled: in forty years with railways, I had never had such an experience. Before it was time to leave, no less than thirty southbound freights had passed that spot, an average of one every eight minutes, and if the northbound hauls were taken into consideration, the action equated to one steam train every five minutes continuously for four hours!

Each morning around 11 o'clock an 'SL6' Class 'Pacific' heads a stopping train southwards from Anshan along the Dalian main line. This eagerly awaited working is seen close to our lineside base at Saddle Mountain.

# Chapter 6

# Steam in the forest

China's narrow gauge forestry lines are especially prevalent in Heilong-jiang Province which has 30 per cent of the country's forest and produces 40 per cent of the nation's industrial timber. The long rakes of timber seen heading southwards along the main line through Manchuria have predominently originated from the 44 forestry bureaus in Heilongjiang Province, over 40 per cent of which is covered in forests of Korean pine, Scots pine, larch and commercial hardwoods such as ash, oak, poplar, elm and birch.

Many of the forestry systems are based around a railway network utilizing 762 mm gauge 0-8-0s built to a basic standard design. In addition to her forestry systems, China has some 1,860 miles (3,000 km) of 762 mm gauge local railways operated by provincial or local government to provide public passenger and freight services. These are quite distinct from the forestry lines and have the function of connecting secondary areas of population and production with China Railways. As Heilongjiang Province has more forestry lines so Henan and Hebei Provinces predominate in local narrow gauge railways, with 1,550 miles (2,500 km) of route mileage in operation.

The 762 mm lines of Henan Province move two million tons of freight a year and a typical 28-ton 0-8-0 ambles along perfectly happily with a 300 ton load. China's Association of Local Railways has recently reported that the average cost per ton kilometre or route mile of these local lines is between a third and a half of the costs of road transport. The lines are easy to construct, need little investment and make use of old rail and low power locomotives. The importance and potential of these systems is further indicated by the fact that in 1983 (the latest figures I could obtain) China's local railways moved 34.4 million tons of freight and carried 12.8 million passengers.

Construction of local railways continues and it is anticipated that by the end of the century 9,300 route miles (15,000 route km) could be in operation. Such thinking underscores the fact that China remains a railway economy and emphasizes the age-long truth — now forgotten in the West — that the railway is the most economical, the safest, the most environmentally kind and the most energy efficient form of land transport. The ability of communities to adapt evenly and efficiently to properly co-ordinated railway systems exposes the humbug, wastefulness and anti-social aspects of the road system.

Motive power on the local railways is predominantly steam, mainly 0-8-0s of slightly differing kinds built in China over the last 25 years and based on the 0-8-0 forestry engines which are in turn descended from a standard Russian design. These locomotives weigh around 28 tons and are rated at 234 hp but a larger standard design rated at 380 hp and weighing 42 tons is believed to have been introduced during the 1970s. These larger locomotives are capable of hauling trains in excess of 500 tons. On the forestry lines, the 28-ton 0-8-0 seems to be the standard type and evidence has recently come to light that they are still being built at the Harbin Forestry Machinery Company's works where six were produced in 1986. This discovery is a perfect example of how enigmatic China can be: it was not until my eighth visit to Harbin that I learned that steam locomotives were actually being built there, so bringing the known total of Chinese works, still producing steam locomotives, to three.

Over 200 locomotives have been produced by Harbin in the last thirty years. However, it has long been my suspicion that other works are also producing steam locomotives particularly for the 762 mm gauge and it is possible that more will be discovered, given China's policy of expanding these lines especially in areas where coal is easily available.

The Harbin Forest Machinery Company also overhauls locomotives and when I took a group to visit the works in 1987, five 0-8-0s were in various stages of shopping whilst a brand new high-capacity tender proudly bearing a 1987 works plate stood resplendently in the works yard. The narrow gauge locomotives from the forestry bureaus of Heilongjiang — in addition to some coalfield examples — come to Harbin mounted on special flat wagons carried in the normal freight trains and it is not unusual to see them either in passing freights or standing in yards.

Lanxiang is the most accessible of China's forestry lines; it lies to the north east of Harbin and can be reached in a comfortable six hours by day train, being located 307 kilometres away on the line to Nancha. A visit to Lanxiang in winter is exhilarating; far from the bustle of big cities, it has the appearance of a holiday resort, especially the Guest House set on the edge of town amid an area of wooded hills. The Guest House overlooks the Forestry Railway's line as it runs into the logging yard and sawmill behind which can be discerned the interchange sidings with China Railways. Lanxiang was established during the late 1930s as a logging town under the Japanese occupation. Today it is owned by the Forestry Bureau which oversees the entire operation including the running of the forest farms and the reafforestation programme, an important part of the operation and one neglected by the Japanese occupiers, much to the detriment of production today

*Lanxiang Forestry Railways' 28 ton 0-8-0 No 033 undergoes a periodic overhaul in the works.*

as many of the prime species take over sixty years to reach maturity.

Lanxiang's railway has 105.5 route miles (170 route km) over which eleven steam locomotives operate. All are standard 0-8-0s of the smaller variety and all are coal burners. They are ostensibly identical despite coming from three separate sources; the Harbin Forest Machinery works, Shijiazhuang Power Machinery plant which lies some 175 miles (283 km) south of Beijing, and Chrzanow of Poland. This standard 762 mm gauge design seems to have penetrated all the known forestry lines, so dispelling fond hopes that these remote systems would harbour vete-

*A loaded log train heads across the metals of the Lanxiang forestry system behind one of its 762 mm gauge 0-8-0s.*

ran locomotives of exotic origin. Even the earlier 600 mm gauge networks which supported many of the original logging operations now seem to have disappeared.

Lanxiang's Forestry System has its own station, locomotive depot and works. The system is extremely busy and our 1987 visit found the entire fleet active with the exception of two engines undergoing overhaul. Most workings are on an out and back basis, but two engines remain allocated within the forest. A passenger train traverses the system each day and provides the only access to certain workers' communities. The coaches are remarkably large for so narrow a gauge and the pugnacious little engines work up a remarkable turn of speed despite the fact that the driving wheel is 600 mm in diameter.

Shortly after leaving Lanxiang, the forestry line runs parallel with the main line with just a river between them. During winter the river freezes solid, enabling photographers to move quickly from one line to the next. From certain vantage points it is possible — should one be lucky enough — to catch a forestry train in the foreground with the 'QJs' clearly visible on an embankment in the background. In addition to the many double headers, some triple-headed 'QJ' combinations are regularly seen on this line. Once the little trains enter the forest, stations and crossing loops occur every few miles and innumerable branches are seen disappearing into the trees.

Many of the Forestry Bureaus are now finding that the cutting areas

*A Russian-built 'J50' Skidder tractor drags the logs from the cutting area to the railhead on the Lanxiang Forestry Bureau line.*

are becoming increasingly distant from the permanent way and it is not unusual for some of the 'J50' tractors to have to drag the logs for an hour or more to the loading point. An electric motor driven winch and pulley system lifts the trunks onto the rail bogies for conveyance to the sawmill. There are no wagons in the accepted sense, the logs are simply slung across bogies placed at each end of the trunks so enabling varying log lengths to be conveyed with ease.

Railways are undoubtedly the ideal form of transport in this environment — not least during heavy winter snows — but as the cutting recedes ever further back there is talk of abandoning the railway in favour of trucking routes. Over recent years Lanxiang's network has been reduced from its original 400 kilometres of main line and in the next four years there are plans to reduce this to 70 kilometres and to have phased out the railway altogether by 1995. Hopefully the trucking threat will be averted for the railway infrastructure is already in place and costs little to maintain. It is to be hoped that any new developments will remain centered around this, for were thousands of Red Star trucks ever to pervade the forests in search of logs it would probably be more in the name of Western ideology than good economic and environmental practice.

For the time being Harbin Forest Machinery works continues to produce new 762 mm gauge locomotives, albeit that many of these are not actually used now for forestry work, going instead to mines, rural

The morning passenger train
from Lanxiang pauses at Juan
Jie station. Notice how the
loaded cars on the right are
formed of free moving bogie
units able to take trunks of any
length.

*Cut logs being loaded into the wagons of China Railways at the exchange sidings in Lanxiang. On the left can be seen the operator of the electric motor used to winch the logs out of the adjacent wood yard. Each wagon is loaded by one such operator.*

railways and other industrial installations in small remote communities.

China's narrow gauge railways, whether for logging, rural or industrial use, offer a whole new area of study and interest for the visitor. Many of the systems are as yet un-documented partly because some forestry bureaus in Heilongjiang Province lie outside the permitted areas for foreign tourists. Hopefully, these railways will survive and hopefully too the rural railways will also be expanded in accordance with the government's recently stated plans. But as China becomes increasingly influenced by Western thinking the threat of mass road transportation, which progressively erodes any properly co-ordinated railway network like a spreading cancer, will provide short term piecemeal justification for closures. It is this blight which threatens China's narrow gauge steam railways, every bit as much as dieselization.

# Chapter 7

# Building tomorrow's locomotives

Never will I forget the emotions experienced upon entering Datong Locomotive Works through a small service door which led into the boiler shop. The sight which confronted me sent me into a trance-like state of disbelief for the vast shop contained twenty boilers in varying stages of construction. Inner and outer fire boxes contrasted with boiler shells, all illuminated and silhouetted in ghostly patterns by the welders' blinding flashes and set to a deafening cacophony of heavy drilling. In an instant the memories came flooding back: Crewe, Derby, Doncaster, Swindon, it mattered not, for I was back again amidst the living vitality of the steam age and something I had suspected for many years was confirmed. Our memories have not deceived us, the steam age was every bit as fabulous as we remember it to be.

Every travel group I have taken to China has experienced similar emotions: we usually have an overnight journey from Beijing to Datong and conversation in the cosy sleeping berths is full of excitement and anticipation. We arrive at dawn and go to the Datong Locomotive Works Guest House for breakfast before proceeding to the works at 9 o'clock. The Guest House, which is full of homely charms, was originally built to accommodate Russian advisers during the 1950s.

Datong is located in the north of Shanxi Province, on the border with Inner Mongolia. The city, which is surrounded by bleak mountains, has a 2,000 year history but today is a thriving industrial town. Built on a sea of high quality coal, Datong has come to industrial prominence in recent times and the locomotive works itself opened in 1959. Since then it has produced over 4,000 'QJs' in addition to various batches of 'JS' Class locomotives. The maximum number of engines produced in any one year is 325. The maximum number produced in one month is 31 — exactly one a day — and this was during the winter of 1983/4 at the time of my first visit.

In 25 years Datong built over half the total of locomotives produced by Crewe in more than a century! Unlike its counterparts in Britain, Datong does not undertake overhauls, it is purely a production plant.

*The ghostly patterns of a 'QJ' Class locomotive's inner fire box during welding operations in the boiler shop at Datong works.*

**Above right** *'JS' assembly in the erecting shop at Datong. The traditional American practice of bolting together cylinders and smoke box saddle are clearly visible in the foreground, as the unit for 'JS' Class No 6604 waits to be craned into position.*

**Right** *Welding operations as a 'QJ' nears completion in the erecting shop at Datong.*

The works area covers half a square mile and has a work force of 8,000, a quarter of whom are young women and many of whom can be seen doing the same work as the men.

The works area splits into two parts: the manufacturing processes and the living and social facilities for the workers. Some 95 per cent of the workers live within the complex, which, in essence, forms a separate community of its own. There are 23 principal shops which merit endless study in all their diversity, for an incredible 2,400 machines, comprised of many types and origin, are in operation. As our guide proudly told us, a 'QJ' consists of 10,000 different parts!

Entering the erecting shop first thing in the morning finds a naked frame over the pits, but during the course of the day that frame evolves into a fully fledged locomotive. I remember standing watching these activities with incredulity and wondering how to describe the scene when our red-blooded Chinese guide turned to me and said — and I'll never forget his words — 'Our workers move like Charlie Chaplin did in your old movies'.

One of the high spots of our visits to Datong has been to meet David Wardale, an expatriate British locomotive engineer who first achieved world acclaim for his rail traction development work in South Africa, particularly with the '26' Class 4-8-4 steam locomotive *Red Devil*. David is currently fulfilling a contract with China Railways to produce

**Right** *The outer firebox shell of a 'JS' receives careful attention from a welder in the boiler shop at Datong.*

**Below** *Spinning steel tyres being heated by jets of flaming coal gas prior to being shrunk onto 'QJ' Class driving wheels at Datong.*

**Far right** *'QJ' Class locomotives under construction in the erecting shop at Datong.*

**Below right** *'QJ' Class driving wheels, with the tyres now firmly shrunk into place, wait to be rolled beneath the giant in the background in the erecting shop at Datong.*

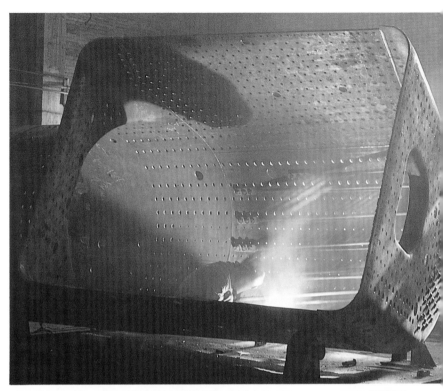

A flamingo-liveried 'JS' Class 2-8-2 receives its first breath of life amid the gloom of the steam testing shed at Datong.

*Productivity poster from Datong Locomotive works.*

modified and new designs, based around the 'QJ'. This work incorporates a range of technical and mechanical improvements, which, in the light of modern practice, can meaningfully be applied to the conventional steam locomotive to increase both its efficiency and power output.

*The welcoming sign at the entrance to the Datong Locomotive Works Hotel.*

*A 'QJ' boiler nearing completion and ready for transfer to the erecting shop at Datong.*

加强安全教育
严禁违章作业

*Hoardings can be seen all around Datong works extolling the workers to read the* Little Red Book of Safety.

David's devotion to the case for steam and his brilliant advocacy have greatly impressed the Chinese, but the crucial question remains, whether his new designs will be built or whether steam will be phased out entirely beyond the early summer of 1988 when the last commissioned batch of 'JSs' is scheduled to be completed. The dilemma centres around the railway bureaus, seventeen out of 22 of which have traditionally used Datong's locomotives, but now request instead powerful diesels. China's past reluctance to produce a bigger and more powerful steam design has led to a strong argument for dieselization. The country's economic expansion and the massive increase in freight traffic this has brought about, and the incapacity of the railway to move this tonnage, has accentuated the demand for extremely powerful locomotives. Diesels seem to offer the most effective way to solve the present problems, rather than any ideological steam versus diesel reasoning.

This situation contrasts with the government's Policy Studies Group, who believe that the on-going use of steam will be beneficial to China, on the basis that the utilization of home resources, such as coal and iron, will reduce China's dependence on oil and her need to import the expensive technology necessary for modern traction. However, in an apparently ever liberalizing China, the railway bureaus now have considerable autonomy and cannot be controlled so easily by central government: the fact is that they are simply not ordering Datong's products.

David feels that if China does embark on a new phase of steam production, it could precipitate some changes of policy in other parts of the world. Certainly China is keen to export — either her existing designs, or others built to required specification — and were she, in addition, to be seen to be able to supply spare parts for steam locomotives around the world, it would be a great benefit to those countries that wish to continue with steam traction but find the provision of spares an increasingly difficult problem in a world where production is almost exclusively centered on other forms of traction.

It is fitting that a British locomotive engineer should be in resi-

*Datong Locomotive Works official catalogue for the 'JS' 2-8-2 'Mikado'.*

dence at this last shrine: that it happens to be in the wilds of Inner Mongolia only serves to heighten the drama. If David's efforts come to fruition, they will be the manifestation of two years' dedicated toil in exile, acting out deep personal beliefs, for this may well be the last attempt to perpetuate the conventional steam locomotive as we know it. In other parts of the world the concept of a totally new order of steam locomotives is being seriously studied. The ACE designs prepared in America are known well enough, but recent news indicates that Soviet scientists are 'inventing the steam engine', having prepared

具有八轮煤水车的QJ型蒸汽机车
QJ-type steam locomotive with 8 wheel tender.

JS型蒸汽机车
JS-type steam locomotive.

专业生产

设计先进

品质优良

**Professional manufacturing**
**Modern designs     Best quality**

具有十二轮煤水车的QJ型蒸汽机车
QJ-type steam locomotive with 12 w

*A page taken from the Datong Locomotive Works' sales booklet depicting products on offer for China's Railway Bureaus and potential export customers (the printing quality of the original brochure does leave something to be desired!)*

*A brace of new 'QJ' 2-10-2s bedecked in their flaming works undercoat bask amid the smoky gloom of the steam testing shed at Datong.*

blueprints for an 8,000 hp solid fuel burning locomotive, which they claim may be three times more efficient than conventional, diesel or electric locomotives. Apparently a prototype is to be built at the locomotive works in Voroshilovgrad. The engine will rely on coal dust or low grade coal and if successful will see service in the coal bearing areas of eastern Russia.

Close to the steam testing shop in Datong stands a solitary reminder of the days when Britain's locomotives ruled the railways of the world in the form of an Edwardian Mogul, designed in the Glasgow suburb of Springburn. How her pretty British aesthetics contrast with the mighty Chinese giants of three quarters of a century later. An exile from the days when Glasgow's ships ruled the world's oceans and her locomotives the world's land masses, this pretty engine had been the works pilot between 1958 and 1962.

Tearing oneself away from the Datong Locomotive Works, it is worth taking a side trip to the Yung Gang Caves, which lie ten miles west of the city. I usually try to lead my travel groups out to these caves which contain over 50,000 Buddhist statues, sculptures which are not only masterpieces of Chinese religious art but constitute one of the most celebrated grottos on earth. The work began during the 5th century after Buddhism spread to China from neighbouring India. The pride of Yung Gang is a 50 ft high Buddha reposing on an 80 ft cliff face.

**Above** *Datong's Glasgow-designed 'Mogul' lying abandoned in the works yard is a likely candidate for China's National Railway Museum which is being established at Shenyang.*

Although much restoration work has been carried out, the grottos remain strikingly authentic, giving the impression of an exotic find which an archeologist has just stumbled upon. Some of the cave faces have collapsed, exposing the statues to the elements and many are incomplete, heads and limbs are missing and the colours badly faded. In an endeavour to preserve this treasure, the authorities have forbidden the use of flash photography at the caves, for they fear that the flashes would further fade the exquisite colours of the carvings.

After visiting Yung Gang, we usually spend the last hour of the day watching 'QJs' haul coal trains away from Datong's marshalling yards. These engines symbolize everything that is excellent in steam

*Above right Another old pilot engine lies abandoned in the form of 'GJ' Class 0-6-0T No 1019 which was built at Taiyuan in 1959. Though of Chinese origin, she is a fairly clear descendant of a typical European industrial design, with more than a hint of German ancestry.*

traction and the speed with which the heavy trains are got on the move reveals that both machine and men are masters of their job — the crews knowing every nuance of the engine's characteristics.

One afternoon during a solo visit to China, I was walking in the garden of Datong Locomotive Works Guest House, admiring the flowers. It was immediately after lunch. An official visiting Datong from the Railway Ministry in Beijing clearly had the same idea and the two of us came face-to-face alongside a large bank of multi-coloured daisies. He spoke perfect English and I described Datong as being the only place in the world still building steam engines. 'Not so', he replied, 'there are other works in China.' He had just time to mention

*One morning on our way up to the Yung Gang grottos we passed this magnificent steam roller, one of several active examples sighted at various times in Datong. She was built at Sxuzhou in Jiangsu Province in 1966.*

Tangshan before his vehicle arrived to take him back to the works. Tangshan was known to have been building steam during the '70's, but the disastrous earthquake of 1976 destroyed much of the works and it was generally believed that building had ceased. The earthquake which registered 7.8 on the Richter scale, occurred during the small hours of 28 July and lasted 23 seconds, but the destruction it caused was unparalleled in modern history. The city was reduced to ruin and the death toll was 242,000 from a population of 1.06 million. It was predicted that Tangshan had been wiped from the face of the earth and the city was compared with Pompeii.

It was impossible to get clear and reliable information about what was happening in Tangshan and the only solution was to go there myself. The city is located in the north eastern part of Hebei Province, some 160 miles (260 km) east of Beijing. I expected the city to have been partly reconstructed but the extent was breathtaking. Tangshan was a new city, with huge multi-storey buildings, capable of withstanding a force eight earthquake, flanking wide modern thoroughfares. The new city was even two-fifths larger than the original one! The main north to south route through Tangshan is called Construction Road; it is 6¼ miles (10 km) long, a much wider thoroughfare than its predecessor and perfectly suited to modern conditions.

Only the Chinese could have rebuilt so vast a city, so superbly,

**Above** *The pride of Yung Gang is this legendary Buddha staring outwards from the cliff face, the original cave entrance having now been eroded away.*

**Below** *Entrance ticket to the Yung Gang grottoes.*

in so short a time and all that remained of that vile night, when virtually all civilian housing and 90 per cent of industrial and public buildings were destroyed, were a dozen ruined sites, preserved as memorials to the dead and to show visitors how, like a phoenix from the ashes, the new Tangshan had arisen from the old. One of these ruins is the

云冈石窟

**THE YUNGANG GROTTOES**

*Smouldering castings lie on the sandy floor at Tangshan Locomotive Works.*

former erecting shop of the locomotive works, from which two thirds of the original 9,000 employees lost their lives. But construction of 'SYs' was continuing, albeit under less than perfect conditions, with eighty engines a year being turned out.

I was able to tour the works with secretary Wang Wenquan. They were much older premises than those I had seen in Datong and the atmosphere even more 19th century. Entering the rough casting shop was like a scene from the 1850s: the workers moved across the earth floor, filling the moulds with sand, as the morning sunlight streamed in through blackened windows. A wagon, bearing a huge ladle of liquid steel, was periodically winched along an inter-shop trackway. The overhead crane picked up the ladle and flitted it across the shop floor, visiting every mould with its fertilizing touch, like a bee flitting from bloom to bloom. In the adjacent shop, mounds of dull grey castings were heaped up amid the gloom, wheels, cylinders and frame sections being immediately recognizable. A deafening blast of heavy drilling indicated that the rough castings were being processed in readiness for subsequent machining. Periodically the ground would tremble, and an explosion shook the entire shop — a hot cylinder casting had been dropped into water, thence to be carried by the overhead crane, still steaming, to join the castings waiting to go to the machining and finishing shops.

In the corner of the castings section stood the carbon convertor,

*Filling castings with liquid steel at Tangshan.*

in which scrap metal and various off-cuts from the works were mixed with limestone to remove the carbon content and produce quality steel. The convertor crackled and threw sparks as it belched black smoke, animated and devil-like in its alchemy. But its demonic climax came at charging time when the top lifted like the shell of a giant sea squid, to reveal four red hot prongs. The overhead crane then fed the monster with bucket loads of scrap and limestone. But in order to drop the substances inside, the bucket's bottom capsized and meshing hung limply silhouetted against the convertor's fiery mouth, giving the appearance of some weird beast from the floor of the deepest ocean. The convertor's top then swung back into place and it began to digest its contents with grunts, shudders, and further sprays of sparks.

In the forges, blackened men flitted amid the gloom, in silhouette as they passed against the ground-shaking thumps of steam hammers of many sizes, pounding the red hot ingots into shape. In the centre of the shop stood one of gargantuan proportions, performing its hypnotic task and exploiting the malleability of a white hot Anshan billet, which it gradually elongated and shaped to form the driving axle of an 'SY' locomotive. Each stroke caused the earth to tremble, and I thought of the mighty hammer which James Naysmyth supplied to the Woolwich Arsenal, the blows from which could be clearly felt at the Greenwich Observatory two miles away. I thought also of James Nays-

*The rough castings of 'SY' Class driving wheels at Tangshan.*

*Stockpiles of 'SY' pony and driving wheels lie in Tangshan works yard prior to being taken to the machining shop.*

myth's visit to the Black Country during the 1840s, described in his autobiography and in particular of a phrase that described the scene before me here: 'smut covered white-eyed men, who dashed between the flames against a roaring cacophony of furnaces and clanging mills'.

In an adjacent shop, I came upon three men manufacturing fire-box rivets. One man drew the pieces of red hot metal from the furnace and placed them in a machine driven by a rapidly revolving fly wheel. The rivets were punched into shape before the machine flung them, still glowing, into a carefully placed wheelbarrow — never missing! The wheelbarrow stood bathed in shafts of smokey sunlight that seeped into the forge. It was Tangshan Locomotive Works in 1986, but it could just as easily have been Beyer Peacock's works in Gorton in 1886 — the

theme was the same, endowed with an industrial timelessness. This was the magic of Tangshan and although the whole operation was archaic, it utilized labour well enough in a centrally planned economy.

Less spectacular were the ordered and considerably quieter machine shops with their huge lathes and masses of machine tools. Here, cylinder castings bolted down the middle in the American manner were being machined to precise tolerances, as were pistons, valves and rubbing surfaces of the axle boxes etc. Nearby, bar frame components were being pressed and bolted into their intricate patterns.

In the boiler shop the inner and outer sections of the firebox are riveted, before moving forwards to receive the barrel sections, which are welded together rather than riveted in the traditional heavy fashion which was so characteristic a practice of British locomotive builders. Welding is far cheaper and, apparently, more durable! As the boiler progresses along the shop, the tube plates are fitted, followed by the tubes themselves. When the boilers arrive at the erecting shop end, the fixing of the superheater elements takes place. Next comes the hydraulic test and simultaneously the boiler receives its flamingo orange undercoat. It is then ready for placing onto an internal rail wagon for transfer to the erecting shop.

There are usually two locomotives in the erecting shop; one almost complete and the other in its early stages. During my stay, I watched an 'SY' grow from the frame stage to the fitting of the cylinders and lowering of the boiler, after which the cab was swung into place. A swarm of workers then descended to complete the fitting up and the entire engine turned into a mass of welders' flashes as the overhead cranes flitted back and forth, bringing all manner of small parts. Welding, bolting or drilling, the men worked rapidly; they knew every action, every screw, every joint and weld. But the most dramatic moment was to come, for as the team completed their finishing touches a set of wheels arrived from the finishing shop and when these had been placed in the 'Mikado' formation, the two overhead cranes combined to lift the locomotive for the shining red wheels to be rolled beneath.

The sheer beauty of seeing a brand new steam locomotive being lowered onto its wheels with a stately momentum is an unforgettable experience, every bit as magnificent as the ceremonial launching of a great ship. All the pieces which have been so carefully forged and machined in the various shops have finally come together to make the finished product and several hours later, the works pilot — a scruffy 'YJ' 2-6-2 — delicately enters the shop and draws the new 'SY', glistening in its flamingo undercoat, from its birthplace into the works yard. Here she joins her tender, which has been welded in unison with the locomotive's progress in the adjacent tender shop. The complete 'SY' is then drawn over to the steam testing shop.

Entering this building is a spine-tingling experience, for it is within its darkened portals that the giants receive their first breath of animation, to stand under steam for 24 hours, with a dozen blue overalled fitters attending to detail ajustments. Soon the new born is moving around the works yard under her own power, with a soft crisp exhaust, ready for the test run on the main line. She will run at full throttle over the 12½ mile (20 km) stretch to Tienzhuang. After proving, the locomotives return to the works to enter the paint shop to acquire their smart black livery, before their rods are taken down and the engines placed in a works siding in readiness to be conveyed to their destination by freight train. Within hours they disappear, so great is China's need for industrial locomotives.

During my stay at Tangshan, I spent some time with Mr Fang Qingfen, the Chief Engineer, and he enthused about the future of steam traction in China. He told me that the Tangshan works have plans to build an improved 'SY', the designs already having been completed.

*Tangshan Works support a wonderful array of vintage machine tools set in a superb 19th century atmosphere.*

He also expressed the hope that Tangshan would eventually export locomotives to other countries, either 'SYs', or specific designs tailored to the recipient's needs. He showed me correspondence with Brazil's Teresa Cristina Railway, along with a photograph of the 'SY2' 'Mikado', which Tangshan had built in 1965 in classic French style, for metre gauge operations in Vietnam. 'We built sixty of them, Mr Qingfen said proudly. His optimism emphasized the tremendous potential which still exists for the steam locomotive in many parts of the world, places where railway operators prefer to use steam, but have allowed themselves to be persuaded otherwise by the major manufacturing nations.

Tangshan's determination to appeal to a world market was declared publicly in the November 1987 issue of the *Railway Gazette* — the inter-

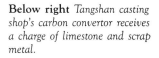

**Below right** *Tangshan casting shop's carbon convertor receives a charge of limestone and scrap metal.*

**Right** *Adding the orange undercoat to a driving wheel prior to assembly.*

**Above right** *Tubeplate welding in the boiler shop at Tangshan.*

**Far right** *Final fitting of superheater elements in the boiler shop at Tangshan prior to hydraulic testing.*

**Right** *A newly completed 'SY' Class 2-8-2 simmers gently in the steam testing shop.*

**Far right** *Tangshan Locomotive Works brochure for the 'SY2' type meter gauge 'Mikado' as supplied to Vietnam. (Again the printing quality of the original brochure is poor by Western standards.)*

national magazine of modern railway technology. In a charming disclosure, headed 'Side Track' and sub-titled 'Steam Dreams', the magazine stated that, 'life in the *Railway Gazette* office was brightened recently by the arrival of a glossy brochure from China's Tangshan Locomotive and Rolling Stock Works, launching an export drive for its 'SY' Class 2-8-2s'. The move has already produced results, as the Valley Railway Corporation in the United States has ordered an 'SY' to haul excursion trains. About a hundred 'SYs' a year are currently being produced at Tangshan and over 1,500 of the class are now in service. The new

中国铁路机车车辆工业公司唐山机车工厂
TANGSHAN LOCOMOTIVE WORKS OF THE
CHINA NATIONAL RAILWAY LOCOMOTIVE AND ROLLING
STOCK INDUSTRY CORPORATION

*Official works photograph of one of the magnificent 'SY2' 'Mikados' built at Tangshan for Vietnam. Note the adherence to the French colonial style, these engines obviously being a close copy of former French exports to French Indo-China.*

brochure gives full details of the design in Chinese and English, and each locomotive comes complete with a Ministry of Railways Certificate for the all-welded boiler and a quality control assurance.

The *Railway Gazette's* remarks are revealing, for no matter how hard headed and technologically minded a railway man might be, the thought of a steam locomotive based on a design of over half a century ago, being rolled off the production line and running round the works yard, whistling and squirting jets of steam, cannot fail to provide a thrill. The very idea offers a regeneration of the spirit: it is as if time itself has been beaten and one's fleeting youthful enthusiasms have been arrested and live again.

# Chapter 8

# The railway people

It is said that there is a bond that links railwaymen across the world: but with the general international decline in railway prestige it often seems as if such links are becoming increasingly tenuous. At one time engine drivers had the social standing afforded to airline pilots today. The railway, in all its variety and social importance, promoted discipline, loyalty and stability. It also provided companionship and a true sense of identity to anyone who was part of the railway family. Many great railwaymen were extremely charismatic and held in awe by their colleagues. As late as the 1950s, I know from personal experience, when working at a large steam depot in Britain, that the appearance of a top-link driver in the enginemen's lobby would almost invariably cause a perceptible hush in the proceedings. It was an involuntary expression of respect from men who were emotionally tough, and not sophisticated or pretentious in any way.

Britain's railways are now regarded as a third rate industry, but to my dying day, I will believe that the decline of Britain's railways, amid the rise of free, uninhibited use of roads has been a fundamental destabilizing force in society and one which has contributed greatly to a decline in social values and an attendant increase in crime. The railway, with its 'permanent way', controls, rather than impedes, man's movements. It is a disciplined form of transport to which man has to relate, it is bigger than the individual and something that he has to respond to in an ordered manner, and that is good for society.

In this final chapter I will introduce you to a few of the railway people it has been my pleasure to meet during my various visits to China, for I have found in them much of the loyalty of service and dedication of spirit, that was once so characteristic a part of Britain's railway industry.

## Zhang Gou-Lu, Chief Engineer of Harbin Steam Locomotive Depot

Mr Zhang is responsible for the maintenance and servicing of Harbin's

120-strong steam fleet, comprised of 'QJs', 'JSs' and 'JFs'. His depot employs a staff of 3,000 and provides locomotives for working the wide range of lines which radiate from Harbin. His duties also embrace the training school and require him to maintain a close liason with the Research Institute of the Harbin Railway Bureau. He is married with two sons, one of ten and one of six years old. Mr Zhang might easily have had a career in the army: he was formal, and remarkably disciplined, both in dress and gait. He was clearly the master of his job and his great ambition now, was to bring about technical improvements to the steam locomotive, not because he believes in it as such, but because he honestly can't envisage a day when China will have no use for them.

Mr Zhang sees the steam locomotive's shortcomings all too clearly, and in his heart he doubts whether it is capable of much improvement in its purest form. He knows that steam traction has disappeared from most other most other parts of the world, but feels that it is beyond China's means to modernize in the forseeable future. He surprised us by stating how much he liked steam traction and he knew that many of his men did too, for although their work was incredibly hard, they felt an affinity with their engines and gained satisfaction from gleaning the best out of them. After all, Mr Zhang continued, 'many of our fathers worked on steam locomotives and we are simply continuing a tradition — I am myself', he confided, 'and that is of great significance in China'.

Mr Zhang was eager to discuss his research work for the Institute; his guinea pig was 'QJ' Class No 291 and the aim was to improve combustion to increase the thermal efficiency and reduce the emmission

*Mr Zhang Gou-Lu, Chief Engineer of Harbin Steam Locomotive depot.*

*Mr Zhang Gou-Lu with his specially modified 'QJ' Class No 291.*

of black smoke. 'If my tests are successful', he said, 'this will solve two of the steam locomotive's inherent weaknesses. Pollution of the atmosphere is becoming an increasingly important issue. People do not like to see dark smoke.'

Rising from his desk, Mr Zhang asked us to follow him, and eagerly he led us through the shed yard to where 'QJ' No 291 stood in light steam. It was marvellous to think that apart from the development work being undertaken at Datong, and Tangshan, other installations around the country — seemingly quite independently — were conducting their own tests. Even if dieselization were to come said Mr Zhang, these tests will continue until we achieve the ultimate goal of an efficient steam locomotive, 'for one day China's oil will be scarce, but our coal will always be plentiful.'

He spoke with strength and vision, for like so many shed masters in China, his face was etched with a rugged determination. Like his colleagues he is a highly capable, emotionally tough man, who sees his greatest talent in life, as keeping China's vast steam communication system in service to the nation.

### Yang Yu-Laing, Depot Master, Three Trees Diesel Depot, Harbin

The depot master met us outside the office building and led us to the meeting room, where bottles of soda-pop awaited us: 'The workers produce this here on the premises', Mr Yang said smilingly, before turning the conversation to his work. 'This depot was built in 1932 for steam locomotives, but was converted to diesel in 1980.' We knew that all passenger trains from Harbin were now diesel-hauled and Mr Yang confirmed this by saying he was responsible for providing locomotives for five major lines; eastward to Mudanjiang, south to Changchun and

*Mr Yang Yu-Laing, Depot Master, Three Trees Diesel Depot, Harbin.*

Shenyang, west to Manzhouli, north west to Wuchang, and northwards to Jamusi.

'Our allocation is 129 engines, more then they have at the steam depot', he said with a chukle, 'and in total we cover 40,000 kilometres a day', which he estimated at some 250 miles (400 km) for each passenger engine. 'We also service four shunting yards', he continued, 'including Sankong.' 'All our duties are performed by two types of locomotive, both with hydraulic transmission; the 'DFH3' and the 'DFH5', the former for passenger, the latter for shunting.' Three Trees undertakes routine servicing of its locomotives every 12,500 miles (20,000 km) and has a staff of 2,200 people, 10 per cent whom are female.

It soon became apparent that the depot was part of a complete railway community, with extensive housing, dining rooms, a hospital, sports grounds, bathing facilities along with a nursery and related playgrounds. Mr Yang was keen to show us round and our first stop was the computer room where all data relating to the depot was assessed, ranging from locomotive mileages and costs to employees' hours and wages. We could not help but agree with Mr Yang's comments about the efficiency of his organization. In almost every corner he made comparisons between conditions at his depot and those at the older steam sheds. Everything at Three Trees was modern, each room was clean and well organized, and throughout the five workshops it seemed that not so much as a tool was out of place. It seemed quite evident that the workers' welfare was a management priority too and Mr Yang confirmed this, saying, 'Close attention to the welfare of the people is the only way to increase efficiency and production.'

For someone in charge of 2,200 workers, Mr Yang was an uncomplicated man. Outwardly very easy going, the invariable smile on his face had an air of mischievous innocence. But he was by his own admission a disciplinarian, possessing the confidence to enact his strong views. He was, he claimed, all the better at his job for having risen through the ranks. At one time, he told us, he had driven 'RM' Class 'Pacifics'. 'Many of our locomotive men come from a steam background,' he continued,'but others have come direct from college.'

Mr Yang was married with three children, two girls and a son. His official working week is 48 hours, eight hours for six days — as it is for the rest of his workforce — but he finds his job so satisfying and motivating, that much of his free time is taken up with extra work, and even when he is at leisure he finds himself reading books on railway management. He summed it up neatly: his work is his life.

It was obvious that the Three Trees Depot worked to an enviable level of efficiency and we asked Mr Yang, what were the main qualities he brought to bear to achieve this and the reply came without hesitation: 1. Correct leadership of the Party. 2. Democratic management. 3. Severe rules and regulations for all to abide by. 4. Workers' welfare. 5. Always looking for progress and improvements.

It was at this point that I was, perhaps surprisingly, struck by the similarities between Mr Yang and shed masters I had known in Britain, for he was clearly a great railway man. He wanted railways to succeed and to work well, to contribute to the economic health of the nation. 'The railway', he 'continued, is China's premier industry. I see the railway network as the vessels of blood in China's body. We must strive for the ultimate modernization of the entire system, not least in replacing steam traction with diesel or electric'. For all this Mr Yang admitted that steam locomotives were cheaper to build and maintain, but he still regarded diesel as superior. He then surprised us by predicting that within the next three years, all passenger trains on China Railways will be either electric or diesel-hauled. He also foresaw the replacement of steam on all heavy long distance freight trains over the next five years. And yet, despite his dedication to future progress and his vision of 'efficiency', he agreed that he would be sad to see the steam locomotive disappear. 'After all', he shrugged with an air of impudent humour, 'I was once a steam driver myself.'

## Shi De Yun, Steam Locomotive Driver, Harbin

Mr Shi De Yun is 41 years old. He is married with one boy and one girl and he lives in a railway house close to the depot. His interests are chess and electric piano. Mr Shi wanted to be an engine driver since being a small boy and in 1964 he entered the Locomotive Drivers' School for Heilonjiang Province and following three years' study became a fireman. Later he became a deputy driver and, having passed the necessary examinations, finally became a driver after many further long years of training.

Mr Shi's regular engine is 'QJ' No 258 and he has driven this engine for eight years. He explained that each locomotive crew consists of three men; a driver, a deputy driver, and fireman and his team is one of four that is associated with engine No 258. The two principal routes for his team are Harbin to the east as far as Yi Mina Po, which is 103 miles (165 km) away and southwards down the main line to Changchun as far as Tao Lai Zhao, 77½ miles (124 km) away. These towns represent the working limits for Harbin's engines over these routes, the crews returning from them with their engine and another train back to Harbin. The shifts can extend to twelve hours and sometimes involve lodging turns if the flow of traffic in the opposite direction is not conducive to a manageable shift.

He readily admitted that his work was tough, dirty and cold, but he enjoyed it, not least, he said, because he knows his job is important to his country. And would he prefer to drive a diesel locomotive? 'Yes', he looks forward to that. 'Every driver hopes to work on a diesel, they will improve our situation greatly.' Dirty the 'QJs' may be, I mused, but I couldn't imagine Mr Shi every getting grimed up, he looked far too smart, almost immaculately dressed for that. I guessed the situation in China to be much as it used to be in Britain, in that some drivers could spend ten hours on a shift and get down from their engine looking almost as fresh as when they had started, whilst other men would be oil smudged and grimy within minutes of mounting the foot-

*Mr Shi De Yun, Steam Locomotive Driver, Harbin.*

plate. Interestingly, at this point, Mr Shi said he honestly didn't know whether steam was better than diesel. It's very difficult to compare them he said, because they both have good and bad points.

One question we were keen to ask Mr Shi was what he thought about seeing foreigners with cameras at the lineside, was he surprised that people came from all over the world to take pictures of steam trains? 'No', he said, he was not surprised at all, he had got used to seeing them and is well aware that many countries no longer have steam trains.

I commented on how varied Harbin's 'QJs' were; some spotless, others dirty, some decorated and some plain. 'Cleanliness is the responsibility of the team,' Mr Shi replied, some drivers it seems are fastidious about maintaining their engines, others less so. 'But there isn't always an opportunity,' he emphasized, 'if we don't stop long enough at stations, or in sidings, there is no chance for cleaning, especially nowadays when our engines are kept moving through seven days a week all round the clock.' He confirmed that the drivers do have a say on the choice of colours used to embellish their locomotives, but the really ornate decorations are awarded by the shed master, for teams who have run one million kilometres in complete safety and without problems.

I was especially keen to ask if some of Harbin's 'QJs' were known to be better performers than others? Yes, we have several noted black sheep in Harbin's allocation; shy steamers, rough riders, sluggish performers. 'And what is No 258 like?' we asked. Mr Shi's face broke into a beaming smile, and he replied 'It is very good!' My final question struck a sad note in an otherwise delightfully happy and good humoured atmosphere. How long did Mr Shi think it would be before diesels appeared on the heavy freights southwards of Changchun? 'Three years,' he answered.

### Lui Tianli, Overhead Crane Driver, Tangshan Locomotive Boiler Shop

Lui Tianli joined Tangshan Locomotive works in 1983. She was following a family tradition, as her father had recently retired from the works. She lives with her parents in a railway house and intends to make the railway her career, even after she is married and has children. Four days a week are spent in the railway college and the other two operating the crane in the boiler shop. I asked if she had found it difficult to operate such large machinery. She laughed, and readily confessed that she did, saying that the job was not only very unfamiliar but that she had also had to overcome a fear of heights.

*Lui Tianli (right), overhead crane driver, Tangshan Locomotive boiler shop.*

She reassured us that she had now overcome this obstacle and settled happily into her job. The boiler shop cranes have a capacity to lift 25 tons and apart from moving components, her job is to lift the

18-ton boiler shells onto wagons for conveyance into the adjacent erecting shop.

Tianli spoke of the tremendous teamwork which existed at Tangshan, partly in response to the disaster, and because of the extra efforts needed to restore production to former levels in conditions which were still far from ideal. 'We have to complete all tasks to the deadline set,' she said, 'and everyone must co-operate and work hard.' In China, the workers are the masters of their country, and she is proud to be part of its development. Pride seemed to come before material reward, pride in contributing to China, their land and the future of their children.

Such stirring sentiments, though undoubtedly influenced by China's socialist doctrines and perhaps partly to impress visitors, nevertheless clearly sprang from the heart and I was reminded of a conversation I had had at Datong with one of the girl workers in the moulding shop. Her name was Duo A Pin, she was 24 and engaged in the repetitive task of placing sand in a particular mould. I remember asking her if she ever felt boredom in the nature of her task. The question clearly surprised her: each part, she said, no matter how small, is integral to the whole. She was helping to build a complete locomotive and those locomotives are helping to build China. She told me how she could see the passing trains from the window of her family's railway apartment and described the pride she felt on seeing the new locomotives hauling their big trains. 'So naturally', she continued, 'I am proud of my work and enjoy it.' A fascinating and sad analogy can be made with the average Western worker, whose reply to such questions of job motivation would be more likely to centre around hours, money and convenience from home, rather than any feeling for the country as a whole.

I asked Tianli if she had a boyfriend; she gave a fleeting smile, blushed, bent her head down and gave a shy nod. Her smile was wonderfully innocent and naive for the girls of China hold a special charm that exudes tremendous power and their constant giggles and laughs are a joy to experience.

As we sat watching a new 'SY' begin its first tentative movements around the works yard, I asked Tianli if it was difficult for her to understand the nature of the foreigner's interest in China's railways. 'For us', she explained, 'steam locomotives and the railway are all around us.' She knew no other way and could not readily understand either our interest, or the concept of the railway ever falling into decline. However, she was astute enough to say that she did see foreign visitors as people who were contributing to the growth of China by publishing books about it and promoting even indirectly tourism and foreign trade.

## Lui Chi Chung, Chief Engineer of Changchun Locomotive Works

Mr Lui was educated at Tangshan Railway College, from which he graduated in 1955 and from where he came directly to Changchun Locomotive Works. He lives in railway accommodation and is married with two children, a boy of 22, also employed at the works, and a girl of 24 who is not in railway service.

In spite of the tremendous responsibility Mr Lui carried, he was remarkably relaxed and cheerful. Changchun is one of China's largest locomotive works, it employs 5,000 people and undertakes 300 major overhauls a year on locomotives which have run 250,000 km (156,250 miles). The main effort concentrates on handling four classes: 'QJ', 'JS',

*Lui Chi Chung, Chief Engineer of Changchun Locomotive Works, standing alongside one of his incentive programme blackboards based on a galactic theme.*

'RM' and 'SL6' but also overhauled here are a few forestry and mine engines of various gauges. No diesel work is undertaken and neither are the works involved in any kind of development work, although Mr Lui did tell us that they had fitted Giesel chimneys to some 'QJs'.

Mr Lui was a man of his people; he was not dictatorial, nor striving to make any particular mark, but seemed rather to lead from within and encourage his workers forward to meet extremely difficult production targets. It was a different style of leadership, and throughout the works, slogans and pictures relating to productivity were to be found. 'These are to encourage our people to work harder,' he explained, 'because in turn, a successful China will work harder for them.' I pointed to a slogan emblazoned over one of the cranes in the erecting shop, and asked him what it said. 'Our work must make the customer satisfied' he replied. Throughout the works — as in many of China's industrial plants — one senses an atmosphere of 'un-stoppability', a compulsion to keep working. The truth of this was revealed by the fact that Mr Lui's works undertake each major overhaul within a period of twenty days from the engine's arrival. The operation is grouped into three principal phases; frame, wheels and boiler.

Mr Lui's smile became increasingly disarming the more he relaxed and he became ever more enthusiastic to talk to us. His major interest apart from his work is meteorology and I had noticed in going around the works, that many of the blackboard slogans and diagrams, impeccably drawn in coloured chalks, featured themes on rockets, outer space and the galaxies, all of which had been carefully constructed to expound some important earth-bound truth in connection with the task in hand. One interesting sequence depicted a 'QJ' and a space rocket and an over simplified interpretation was that if the 'QJ' was overhauled well, it would enable China to be great, and one day to reach the galaxies.

I took the opportunity to ask Mr Lui to confirm my suspicion that the boilers of the 'RM' 'Pacifics' and 'JS' 'Mikados' were interchangeable. 'They are', he answered, 'but that is irrelevant because we don't change the boiler of any individual engine.' He continued to explain that depot managers and engine crews all insisted on the original boiler being returned with the locomotive. Presumably this is for the crews to maintain their chosen colours and embellishments, along with any safety awards allocated to them. I could only wonder how overhauls could be enacted so swiftly without the facility to change boilers. It is certainly a remarkable practice in a country which is as time and production conscious as China.

As Mr Lui's meteorites indicated, he believed in progress and took a long view of the future. But he saw an immediate need for the diesel. 'The steam locomotive's thermal efficiency is so very low,' he said, 'less than 8 per cent of the latent energy is used in traction, whereas in the diesel it is 20 per cent'. Mr Lui's clarity of vision for tomorrow permitted no sentiment for the past, and no sadness for the demise of steam. Any room for such forebodings was dissipated in the all consuming

*Incentive schemes for the workers by the score.*

glow of his vision for China's future, a future that will need the railways and, for the present at least, the products of Harbin, Datong and Tangshan to help the nation to reach the stars.

Details 'of Colin Garratt's tours to China can be obtained from:

Occidor Ltd,
10, Broomcroft Road,
Bognor Regis,
West Sussex
PO22 7NJ.
Telephone: 024369 2178


Details of Colin Garratt's other publications, Video releases, and Audio Visual shows, are available from:

Monica Gladdle,
Carlestrough Cottage,
Shangton Road,
Tur Langton,
Leicestershire.
LE5 0PN.
Telephone: 085884 438.

# Index